# The Young Learner's™
# Bible Storybook

DR. MARY MANZ SIMON

# The Young Learner's™ Bible Storybook

## 52 Stories • Over 100 Activities

ILLUSTRATED BY PIERS HARPER

**Standard Publishing**

cincinnati, ohio

© 2002 Mary Manz Simon
© 2002 Standard Publishing, Cincinnati, Ohio
A division of Standex International Corporation
All rights reserved.
Sprout logo is a trademark of Standard Publishing.
Printed in Italy.

08  07  06  05  04  03          9  8  7  6  5  4

Project editors: Lise Caldwell, Jennifer Holder
Graphic design and art direction: Robert Glover
Production director: Linda Ford
Typesetting: Andrew Quach

ISBN 0-7847-1277-8

Scripture quotations marked *(CEV)* are taken from the *Holy Bible, Contemporary English Version.* Copyright © 1995 by American Bible Society. Used by permission.

Scripture on back cover and other Scripture quotations marked *(NIV)* are taken from the *HOLY BIBLE, NEW INTERNATIONAL VERSION. NIV.* Copyright 1973, 1978, 1984 by International Bible Society. Used by permission of Zondervan Publishing House. All rights reserved.

Scriptures marked *(ICB)* are taken from the *International Children's Bible® New Century Version®.* Copyright © 1986, 1988, 1999 by Tommy Nelson™, a division of Thomas Nelson, Inc., Nashville, Tennessee 37214. Used by permission.

Library of Congress Cataloging-in-Publication Data

Simon, Mary Manz, 1948-
    The young learner's Bible storybook : 52 stories with activities for family fun and
learning / written by Mary Manz Simon ; illustrated by Piers Harper.
        p. cm.
    Summary: A collection of Bible stories for young children accompanied by memory
verses, games, songs, and activities related to the featured concepts.
    ISBN 0-7847-1277-8
    1. Bible stories, English. 2. Christian education—Activity programs. [1. Bible stories. 2.
Bible games and puzzles.] I. Harper, Piers, ill. II. Title.

BS551.3 .S56 2002
220.9'505—dc21

                                                                    2002018707

from Mary
*For Hank*
*1 Corinthians 13:13*

from Piers
*For Daniel and Nicholas*

# Table of Contents

# Dear Parents,

Time is one of the greatest gifts we give to our children. They might beg for the latest toy or whine for a snack before supper, but most of all, children want our time and attention, a lap and our love.

## Savor the time today

So now, we shiver on the sidelines of a soccer game. Years later, our faithfulness is forgotten, but our child grows up feeling valued. We lose sleep to comfort a feverish preschooler. Years later, the anxious nights are forgotten, but our child grows up with a sense of security. And as we share God's story, a young child might giggle as we attempt to pronounce "Methuselah," but he grows up knowing that God loves him. Today we share the time; tomorrow we savor the memories.

*The Young Learner's Bible Storybook* can make the time you share and the memories you build with your child even more meaningful. The stories and activities are fun and filled with valuable lessons. As an educator, mother, and author, I respect and value your role in helping your child learn.

## Young children think concretely

Core values and biblical truths come to life in what we say, how we live, and what we do every day. That's because a young child thinks concretely. He lives and thinks in the here and now. A six year old doesn't imagine what it means to be honest; he knows what it means because he heard you talk with the police officer who caught you speeding. And a four year old isn't puzzled by the true meaning of Christmas; he blows out the candles on Jesus' birthday cake.

## Your teaching is relevant

He also learns about the world from you. He knows the difference between up and down. He knows that the sky is blue and that ice feels cold, because you have been his first teacher.

Your teaching is developmentally appropriate because you are an expert on the child you love. Your teaching is relevant because lessons happen naturally at the grocery store, in the kitchen, and with a storybook at bedtime. Because you know your child, your teaching connects with both his head and his heart. *The Young Learner's Bible Storybook* will give you more opportunities for teaching and make the task even easier.

## Here are suggestions to maximize your time:

1. Several elements are provided for each story, but you don't need to use them all at once. For example, you might read the story and talk about the illustrations one day, sing a song another day, and do another activity a day (or a week) later.

2. When we spend time learning about Jesus, we communicate that growing as a Christian is a lifelong process. That's why I encourage you and your child to discuss the topics that naturally emerge. You don't need to be a perfect teacher with all the answers!

3. The variety of formats and activities in *The Young Learner's Bible Storybook* reflect that children learn by being mentally and physically active. That's the reason your child will be asked to listen attentively to fill in the blanks when you read "A Small Brown Donkey," and to stand up and sit down in the story, "Up a Tree." The combination of thinking and doing helps your child remember the Bible story, Bible concept, and the early learning concept.

4. Some of the fifty-two stories in *The Young Learner's Bible Storybook* retell only a small portion of the biblical narrative. For example, in "Songs From Prison," the emphasis is on the faith Paul and Silas have in God, not on their suffering. The abstract elements and complicated details in some Bible stories begin to make sense only as children grow older. Stories included in *The Young Learner's Bible Storybook* are developmentally appropriate for children from about three to seven years of age.

5. Some of the stories, such as the creation story, will be familiar. Other stories, such as the building of Solomon's temple, may be less well-known. But all the stories present truths that are as relevant today as when they were originally recorded. Even in today's world of virtual reality, children crave authenticity. In *The Young Learner's Bible Storybook*, you and your child will read about real people and our real God.

When a child learns about Jesus at an early age, he spends a lifetime walking with the Savior. When a child gains early learning skills, he has a solid foundation on which to build for the future. When you share God's Word with your child, God promises to bless your time together.

*Dr. Mary Manz Simon*

# Old Testament Stories

# The First Seven Days

**BIBLE TRUTH**
God created
the world.

**LEARNING FUN**
Visual recognition of
numerals 1–7

**SCRIPTURE REFERENCE**
Genesis 1:1–2:3

**MEMORY VERSE**
"He is the God who made
the whole world and
everything in it."
*Acts 17:24, ICB*

Encourage your child to repeat the entire second
line of each section, or just the words, "It is good."

Long, long ago, God created the world.
Here is how it happened:

On Day **1**, God created light.
*God looked at what he created and said,
"It is good."*

On Day **2**, God created the sky above
the earth.
*God looked at what he created and said,
"It is good."*

On Day **3**, God created the oceans
and flowers and trees.
*God looked at what he created and said,
"It is good."*

On Day **4**, God created the moon,
the stars, and the sun.
*God looked at what he created and said,
"It is good."*

On Day **5**, God created the birds and the fish.
*God looked at what he created and said, "It is good."*

On Day **6**, God created animals and people.
*God looked at what he created and said, "It is very good."*

On Day **7**, God rested.

# Activities

## To the **parent**

Throughout your day, teach your child about God's creation. A young child will embrace the simple fact that "God created the world." When a child teases, "Did God create the tarantulas? The worms? The fireflies?" he usually wants to verify his understanding. Patient reinforcement will emphasize the fact that God made the world.

## Game to **play**

Write each numeral from 1–7 on an index card or a sticky note. Place the cards or notes on or near the corresponding number of objects around your house or your child's room. Then have a "Numeral Scavenger Hunt" and encourage your child to find each number and show it to you or tell you which objects it corresponds to ("I found 6 marbles!"). Play this game over the course of a few minutes, hours, or days.

## Song to **sing**

*Sing "He's Got the Whole World in His Hands" together.*

He's got the whole world in his hands,
He's got the whole, wide world in his hands,
He's got the whole world in his hands,
He's got the whole world in his hands.

He's got the wind and the rain in his hands . . .
He's got you and me in his hands . . .
He's got everybody in his hands . . .

## Verse to **say**

"He is the God who made the whole world and everything in it." *Acts 17:24, ICB*

## Prayer to **pray**

Dear God, I know that you are great. You created the whole world. Amen.

# Two by Two

**BIBLE TRUTH**
God cares for us.

**LEARNING FUN**
A pair is two matched items

**SCRIPTURE REFERENCE**
Genesis 7:1-8:18

**MEMORY VERSE**
"The Lord is good. He protects those who trust him in times of trouble."
*Nahum 1:7, CEV*

God told his plans to this old man –
"Now, Noah, build a boat.
Build it so high, build it so wide,
and then your boat will float.

"A big, big rain will start to fall
and last a long, long time.
That rain will cover all the earth,
but inside you'll be fine.

"Now take along some animals.
I'll bring them two by two;
then when I've gathered all the pairs,
you'll have a floating zoo.

"Old Noah, you will be all right,
your wife and children, too."
"God, I will trust you," Noah said.
"I'll build your floating zoo."

Two rhinos are a pair of beasts;
two snakes, they make a pair.
Two elephants will be quite large –
some space they'll need to share.

The doors soon closed on Noah and
the beasts all, two by two.
The raindrops then began to fall
upon the crowded zoo.

Inside the boat the pairs had fun.
They wiggled, squiggled, flew –
the pairs that Noah brought inside,
that marched in two by two.

The rain then stopped, the sun came out,
the flood soon dried up, too.
The animals marched off the ark
in pairs of two by two.

#  Activities

A child who grows up in a language-rich environment naturally builds a vocabulary of words. But an adult must help the child build a vocabulary of mathematics-related concepts, such as the word "pair," which is used in this story. When you shop, say, "Let's buy a *pair* of shoes" or "We need to find a *pair* of mittens." This will help your child relate the concept of "two" to "a pair." Informally test your child's understanding by asking questions such as, "Why are sunglasses called a pair?"

## Game to **play**

*Wear a pair! Have fun asking and answering these "pair" questions.*

When it's snowy outside, what pair do you wear on your feet?

When you want to protect your eyes from the sun, what pair do you wear on your nose?

Before you put on your shoes, what pair do you wear?

When you want to make a snowball, what pair do you wear on your hands?

When you walk on a hot, sunny beach, what pair do you wear on your feet?

# Song to **Sing**

*Sing "Arky, Arky" together.*

The Lord told Noah, "There's gonna be a floody, floody." (repeat)
Get those animals out of the muddy, muddy, children of the Lord.

> (chorus)
> So rise and shine, and give God the glory, glory.
> Rise and shine and give God the glory, glory,
> Rise and shine and give God the glory, glory,
> Children of the Lord.

The Lord told Noah to build him an arky, arky. (repeat)
Build it out of hickory barky, barky, children of the Lord.

> (chorus)

The animals, the animals, they came in by twosies, twosies. (repeat)
Elephants and kangaroosies, roosies, children of the Lord.

> (chorus)

It rained and poured for forty daysies, daysies. (repeat)
Almost drove those animals crazy, crazy, children of the Lord.

> (chorus)

# Verse to **Say**

"The Lord is good. He protects those who trust him in times of trouble." *Nahum 1:7, CEV*

# Prayer to **pray**

Dear God, I know you will take care of me. Amen.

# Up and Down Tower

**BIBLE TRUTH**
God alone is great.

**LEARNING FUN**
Directions: up and down

**SCRIPTURE REFERENCE**
Genesis 11:1-9

**MEMORY VERSE**
"Great is the Lord, and most worthy of praise."
*Psalm 48:1, NIV*

As you read this story, say and point "up" each time you see ↑ and point "down" when you see ↓. Encourage your child to point with you.

Let's show everyone how great we are," said one man, flexing his muscles.

"That's a wonderful idea," agreed his friend. "We are pretty great. But how can people see our greatness?"

"We can build a tower that will reach ↑ to heaven," said another. "That will make us famous."

The people agreed. Building a high tower would show everyone how great they were. So the people started to make the bricks. They stacked ↑ the bricks and the tower grew.

"Build it ↑," boomed one of the workers. "The farther ↑ it goes, the greater people will say we are!"

They made more bricks. They stacked ↑ more bricks.
Each day the tower grew ↑ a little higher.

And each day, God grew a little more unhappy with them.
God was sorry that the people bragged about their
greatness. They had forgotten that God was great.
To remind the people of his power, God confused their
language.

"Dibble, dubble?" said one man.

"Craw, craw, tibble?" said another.

One worker stacked a brick on someone's hand. Another
man backed up into a wall and the wall tumbled ↓ .

"Skitter scam tripple?" said another. No one could
understand what the next person was saying. Everyone
was confused.

The tower didn't go ↑ any higher, because the people could not work together to build it. After a while, the people scattered to many different places. The tower started to fall ↓. Years later, only a pile of bricks was left ↑ at the place named "Babel," which means "confused."

# Activities

## To the parent

"Up" and "down" are some of the earliest concepts a baby experiences. Because he is physically involved in learning what these words mean, and he especially likes the cuddling associated with being picked up, "up" is often one of the first words in a toddler's vocabulary.

## Game to play

*Say to your child, "Because the people thought they were greater than God, God confused their languages. The people couldn't understand each other or work together. Sometimes when our tongues get twisted, we babble, too." Have fun trying these tongue twisters. Say each phrase out loud and then ask your child to join you.*

Babel, Bible, Babel, Bible, Babel, Bible, Babel, Bible

goofy great, goofy great, goofy great, goofy great, goofy great

tower tall, tower tall, tower tall, tower tall

brick bake, brick bake, brick bake, brick bake

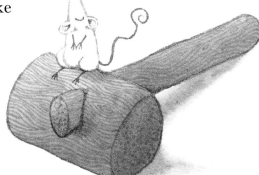

## Questions to a**s**k

*Ask your child to respond to the following questions. Encourage him to point up or down when he answers.*

Do you reach up or do you bend down to
- pick up a toy?
- brush your hair?
- put on your shoes?
- swat a bee?
- hug a cousin?
- climb a jungle gym?
- hang a coat in the closet?

## Verse to **s**ay

"Great is the Lord, and most worthy of praise." *Psalm 48:1, NIV*

## Prayer to **pray**

Dear God, you are great. Amen.

# God's Promise in the Night

**BIBLE TRUTH**
God keeps his promises.

**LEARNING FUN**
Positional prepositions

**SCRIPTURE REFERENCE**
Genesis 15:5, 6

**MEMORY VERSE**
"The Lord has done what he promised."
*1 Kings 8:20, CEV*

**O**utside the tent,
**in** the cool, cool air,
**between** the campfires,
**next to** a tree,
God spoke to Abraham.

**Under** the stars,
**beneath** the bright moon,
**in front of** the rocky hill,
**near** a fast-flowing stream,
God said to Abraham:

"**Above** in the sky,
**beyond** where you can reach,
**farther** than you can imagine,
the stars shine.
Can you count them?

"I promise you, Abraham,
you will have as many children
as there are stars in this
night's sky.

"I will give you a son.
I will give you this country,
and his children will live here."

**Outside** the tent,
**in** the cool, cool air,
**between** the campfires,
**next to** a tree,
Abraham heard God speak.

**Under** the stars,
**beneath** the bright moon,
**in front of** the rocky hill,
**near** a fast-flowing stream,
Abraham knew God would
keep his promise.

# Activities

## To the parent

Young children can learn about prepositions during everyday activities. Enrich your child's vocabulary and encourage the development of good listening skills by giving specific directions. For example, "Put those beach shoes *next to* the tennis shoes," or "Keep your feet *under* the table."

## Game to play

*Play "Simon Says" using these prepositional phrases, or make up your own.*

Simon says (or doesn't say):
- Put your hand *under* your chin.
- Step *over* the toy.
- Sit *on* the floor.
- Put your arms *beside* your body.
- Crawl *between* my legs.
- Put your hands *in* your pockets.

## Song to sing

*Sing to the tune of "Twinkle, Twinkle Little Star."*

Twinkle, twinkle little star,
I can see you near and far,
way up in the sky at night,
sparkling with your lovely light.
When I see your shining glow,
I'm reminded what I know.

Twinkle, twinkle little star,
we show God's love where we are.
You are in the sky so high,
floating in the dark, night sky.
I show God's love where I am;
I know I am Jesus' lamb.

Twinkle, twinkle every night,
you reflect God's perfect light.
God does just what he has said.
Each night when I go to bed,
God has promised me I know:
He will always love me so.

## Verse to say

"The Lord has done what he promised." *1 Kings 8:20, CEV*

## Prayer to pray

Dear God, I know you keep your promises. Amen.

# The Woman Said, "I Will Go"

Help your child find the words "come" and "go" in the text of this story.

**BIBLE TRUTH**
God answers prayers.

**LEARNING FUN**
Visual identification of the words "come" and "go"

**SCRIPTURE REFERENCE**
Genesis 24:1-58

**MEMORY VERSE**
"The Lord . . . answers the prayers of all who obey him."
Proverbs 15:29, CEV

Old man Abraham told his servant, "Go. Find my son a wife."

The servant asked, "What if the woman will not come?"

"God's angel will go ahead of you," said Abraham. "The woman will come."

After the long journey, the servant and his camels rested by a well. The servant prayed, "Dear God, please let the right woman come to the well. I want to go home with a wife for Abraham's son. If I ask a woman for a drink, let her say that she will give water to my camels, also. Then I will know she is the woman who should come with me."

Soon, the servant saw a young woman come to the well. Her name was Rebekah. "Would you get me a drink of water?" the servant asked.

Rebekah said, "Yes, and I will give you water for your camels, also."

Then the servant said to Rebekah, "Come here. I want to thank you for your kindness." The servant gave her two large gold bracelets and a gold ring.

Then the servant said, "May I go home with you? Does your father have a place where my camels and I can sleep?"

Rebekah said, "Of course you may come. Let's go home."

The servant knew God had answered his prayer. God had chosen Rebekah to marry Abraham's son. The servant talked with her family. They all knew God had led the servant to this place.

The next morning, the servant told Rebekah, "It is time to go. Will you come?"

And Rebekah said, "Yes, I will come."

# Activities

## To the **parent**

"Come" and "go" are among the first words a child learns to read because they are so familiar. They are used every day and are actions a child understands at an early age. In addition, the initial letters "c" and "g" are easy for a child to pronounce. Help your child find the words "come" and "go" in the text of this story. This visual identification of simple words, or building a "sight vocabulary," is part of the early reading process.

## Game to **play**

Print the words "come" and "go" on two pieces of paper. When you hold up the word "come," your child should come toward you. When you hold up the word "go," your child should go back to his starting point. Then let your child hold up the words for you and other family members.

## Questions to ask

*Take a few moments to talk with your child about his prayers. What has he prayed for? What have you as a family prayed for? How has God answered those prayers?*

What might you pray
- when a friend is sick?
- when you are thankful for a new toy or book?
- when you are spending a night at someone else's house?
- when you have hurt a friend's feelings?

## Verse to say

"The Lord . . . answers the prayers of all who obey him." *Proverbs 15:29, CEV*

## Prayer to pray

Dear God, thank you for answering my prayers. Amen.

# Ladder to Heaven

**BIBLE TRUTH**
God is with us.

**LEARNING FUN**
Opposites: up and down

**SCRIPTURE REFERENCE**
Genesis 28:10-22

**MEMORY VERSE**
"The Lord Almighty
is with us." *Psalm 46:11, NIV*

Jacob said,

"The sun has gone **down**,
but where will I sleep?
Go **up** on the hill,
or **down** by the creek?

"A rock's over there
close by the creek bed.
That is a good place
To lay **down** my head."

So Jacob lay **down**.
He fell fast asleep,
and dreamed a long dream,
as he snored so deep.

He saw a ladder
that reached **up** so high.
The angels came **down**
from **up** in the sky.

And who was above
so far in the sky?

The King of us all,
our God, the Most High.

Now later that day,
when Jacob got **up**,
he slowly poured oil
into a small cup.

He poured the cupful
**down** onto the ground
right where he had slept
with angels around.

"For Bethel is what
I label this space.
I saw my God here –
it's a holy place."

And so Jacob left.
He went on his way,
but never forgot
what he learned that day.

He'd seen the angels
go **up** and go **down**,
and God also came
right **down** on the ground.

"God will be with me
wherever I go.
That's what I learned here –
I always will know."

God was at Bethel,
but not only there –
God's with us here now
today, everywhere.

# Activities

Long ago, people thought God was only in certain holy places. But God has promised to be with us wherever we are. That thought can be especially comforting to children who are afraid of the dark or feel alone when facing new situations.

## Game to play

Show how you would
- climb up to the top bunk.
- go down to the bottom of the ocean.
- raise a flag up.
- go down to the basement.
- fly up through the clouds.
- go down to the first floor of a tall building.
- reach the top of a slide.

## Questions to ask

*Encourage your child to shout "Yes!" after each pair of questions.*

Is God with you when you sleep?
When you cry and weep?

Is God with you when you pet your dog?
When you catch a frog?

Is God with you when you are alone?
When you talk on the phone?

Is God with you when you are at school?
When you swim at the pool?

Is God with you when you are small?
When you grow tall?

## Verse to say

"The Lord Almighty is with us." *Psalm 46:11, NIV*

## Prayer to pray

Dear God, help me remember that you are with me wherever I go. Amen.

# Dream, Dream, What Does It Mean?

**BIBLE TRUTH**
Only God understands everything.

**LEARNING FUN**
We all dream dreams

**SCRIPTURE REFERENCE**
Genesis 40, 41

**MEMORY VERSE**
"[God] does great things beyond our understanding."
Job 37:5, NIV

The baker had a dream.
He asked Joseph,
"Joseph, Joseph, what does it mean?
Can you understand my dream?"

Joseph said,
"No, I'm sorry, Baker Man,
but God will help me and **he** can."

And God helped Joseph explain the baker's dream.

The king's servant had a dream.
He asked Joseph,
"Joseph, Joseph, what does it mean?
Can you understand my dream?"

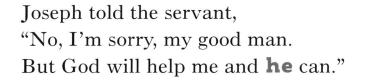

Joseph told the servant,
"No, I'm sorry, my good man.
But God will help me and **he** can."

God helped Joseph explain the
servant's dream.

The king had a dream, and he asked Joseph,
"Joseph, Joseph, what does it mean?
Can you understand my dream?"

Joseph told the king,
"No, King, no. I'm just a man.
But God will help me and **he** can."

And God helped Joseph explain the king's dream.

# Activities

## To the parent

**We all dream. That simple statement may not appear so matter-of-fact to a young child. During the early years, a young child is just learning to distinguish between what is real and what is make-believe. Dreams complicate the issue because a young child sees that his dreams often have elements of both reality and fantasy. Use the fill-in-the-blank prompts below to share your dreams and help your child talk about his dreams.**

## To talk about

Some people dream when they are awake. This is called daydreaming. I like to daydream about _____.

All of us dream while we sleep, but we don't always remember our dreams. I'm glad I don't remember all my dreams, because _____.

Bad or scary dreams are called nightmares. Nightmares seldom happen. I had a scary dream about _____.

Dreaming can be fun. We can imagine wonderful things such as _____.

Even though I can't remember all my dreams, God can. When I think about God knowing what I think and dream I feel _____.

# Song to Sing

*Sing to the tune of "Three Blind Mice."*

*verse 1*
Dream, baker, dream.
Dream, baker, dream.
What does it mean?
What does it mean?
What have you seen in your head at night?
What dream has given you fear and fright?
Will you ask Joseph what meaning it might
have for your life? For your life?

*verse 2*
Dream, servant, dream. . . .

*verse 3*
Dream, King, dream. . . .

# Verse to say

"[God] does great things beyond our understanding." *Job 37:5, NIV*

# Prayer to pray

Dear God, sometimes when I dream, I don't know what things mean. Remind me, God, that you understand everything. Amen.

# A Baby in a Basket

## BIBLE TRUTH
God protects us.

## LEARNING FUN
Auditory discrimination

## SCRIPTURE REFERENCE
Exodus 2:1-9

## MEMORY VERSE
"The Lord protects his people by holding them in his arms now and forever."
*Psalm 125:2, CEV*

**Encourage your child to identify each sound when asked.**

Miriam loved cuddling her little brother. Every day, she helped her mother care for the baby.

"Waah, waah,"
What was that sound?

The crying of the baby startled Miriam. When her brother was tiny, his cries were soft. But now that he was three months old, he was noisier.

Tromp, tromp, tromp.
What was that sound?

The stomping of the soldiers outside signaled danger. Soldiers captured and took away every baby boy they could find.

Swish, swish, swish.
**What was that sound?**

The plant stalks that Miriam's mother brought from the river were ready to use. Miriam and her mother would make a little basket for the baby. They hoped God would protect the baby so he could float to safety.

Splash, splash, splash.
**What was that sound?**

The water lapped against the sides of the basket floating down the river. Along the shore, Miriam watched where the basket went.

"Waah, waah,"
**What was that sound?**

The cries of the baby were heard by a princess bathing. "Oh, what a precious baby boy," she said. "Who will help me care for him?"

Miriam said. "I know a woman who will help you with the baby."

The princess smiled and nodded, "That would be wonderful."

"Gurgle, gurgle, gurgle."
What was that sound?

The happy noises of baby Moses delighted his sister and mother, who helped the princess care for the little boy. God protected baby Moses!

# Activities

Learning that sounds other than language have meaning or give information is one of the auditory discrimination skills a child develops. Help your child identify specific sounds around him. For example, a child might listen and label the sound of water running in the sink, the computer turning on, the crunch of dry leaves, or squirrels chattering outside. Building baseline auditory discrimination abilities will give a child a solid foundation on which he can add skills related to reading and spelling.

## Rhyme to **say**

*Encourage your child to form a basket with his arms and rock the "basket" back and forth as you read.*

Baby Moses in the basket,
you are hidden here,
safe away from Pharaoh's soldiers,
do not fret or fear.

Baby Moses on the river,
God is guarding you.
As you float nearby the palace,
watch what he will do.

Baby Moses at the palace,
you are in God's hand.
You will grow to lead God's people
to the promised land.

## Song to **sing**

*Sing "God Is So Good" together.*

God is so good,
God is so good,
God is so good,
He's so good to me.

He cares for me,
He cares for me,
He cares for me,
He's so good to me.

## Verse to **say**

"The Lord protects his people by holding them in his arms now and forever."
*Psalm 125:2, CEV*

## Prayer to **pray**

Dear God, thank you for watching over baby Moses and thank you for watching over me. Amen.

# The Yes-No King

As you read the story, encourage your child to shake his head no or nod his head yes as indicated.

**BIBLE TRUTH**
We should obey God.

**LEARNING FUN**
Listening vocabulary

**SCRIPTURE REFERENCE**
Exodus 6–12

**MEMORY VERSE**
"If you obey the Lord, he will watch over you and answer your prayers."
*Psalm 34:15, CEV*

God told Moses, "Take my people to the promised land." So Moses told the king, "God wants me to take his people to the promised land."

The king shook his head. **"No.** You can't go."

Moses said, "King, you'll be sorry for not obeying God." The king just laughed.

So God sent frogs to punish the king. Frogs jumped everywhere, and the king was sorry. He nodded. **"Yes,** you may go." But when the frogs were gone the king changed his mind. He said, **"No, no, no.** You can't go."

Moses said, "King, you'll be sorry for not obeying God."
The king just laughed.

So God sent teeny tiny flies to punish the king. Teeny tiny
flies flew everywhere, and the king was sorry. He nodded.
**"Yes,** you may go." But when the teeny tiny flies were
gone the king changed his mind. He said, **"No, no, no.**
You can't go."

Moses went again to the king and said,
"God wants me to take his people to the promised land."

The king shook his head. **"No.** You can't go."

Moses said, "King, you'll be sorry for not obeying God."
The king just laughed.

So God sent a hailstorm to punish the king. Pieces of ice fell from the sky and the king was sorry. He nodded. **"Yes,** you may go." But when the hail was gone the king changed his mind. He said, **"No, no, no.** You can't go."

Again and again Moses went to the king. Again and again the king nodded **yes.** Again and again the king changed his mind and shook his head **no.**

Finally, God sent one terrible punishment. The sorry king nodded. **"Yes,** you may go."

Finally, Moses said, "Today we will leave the **yes-no** king. Today, God's people will leave for the promised land. Hooray!"

# Activities

## To the parent

Even before a baby says the word or a child reads the word, he recognizes the meaning of "No." Throughout the early childhood years, a listening vocabulary contains more words than the reading or speaking vocabulary. Talking with adults offers a child the opportunity to learn word meanings in a real-world context. Conversations can be adjusted to the child's level of understanding. For example, in this lesson, if a child is unsure about the meaning of "punishment," the adult might say, "The king didn't obey God. That's why God sent all those frogs. It's like when you didn't put your dirty clothes in the hamper last night, you couldn't watch television. Not watching TV was your punishment." Watch your child's expressions and nonverbal clues to identify opportunities for defining words.

## Game to play

*Help build your child's listening vocabulary! Read the following sentences to your child, and ask him to guess what the italicized words mean. Feel free to provide hints until your child can guess the meaning.*

Please *deflate* the beach ball so it will fit in the suitcase.
There will be lots of food on the *buffet*.
Put your *contribution* for the offering in the envelope.
We can buy popcorn during the *intermission*.
Let's plant the *annuals* here.
Ask the clerk at the *register*.
You can jump rope at *recess*.
We can see the new *exhibition* at the museum.
Here's a *brochure* about the new church.

# Song to **Sing**

*Sing to the tune of "London Bridge Is Falling Down."*

When I follow all the rules, all the rules, all the rules,
When I follow all the rules, I obey.

Even when no one's around, I'm alone, I'm alone,
Even when no one's around, I obey.

I do what I know is right, know is right, know is right.
I do what I know is right. I obey.

Jesus wants me to obey, to obey, to obey.
Jesus wants me to obey every day.

# Verse to **say**

"If you obey the Lord, he will watch over you and answer your prayers."
*Psalm 34:15, CEV*

# Prayer to **pray**

Dear God, when I find it hard to obey, and make mistakes during the day,
"Forgive me, God" are words I say, and next time help me to obey. Amen.

# Bread From Heaven

**BIBLE TRUTH**
God gives us what
we need.

**LEARNING FUN**
Rhyming words

**SCRIPTURE REFERENCE**
Exodus 16:1-26

**MEMORY VERSE**
"God can bless you with
everything you need."
*2 Corinthians 9:8, CEV*

Where is some food, Moses?"
God's people said.
"We must have food
or we'll soon all be dead.
We wander around;
we're hungry each day.
So Moses come here,
now what do you say?"

The leader of God's group
stood up above all.
He nodded and said,
"Our God's heard you call.
He's God of the earth
and here with us, too.
He loves us and cares,
so here's what he'll do.

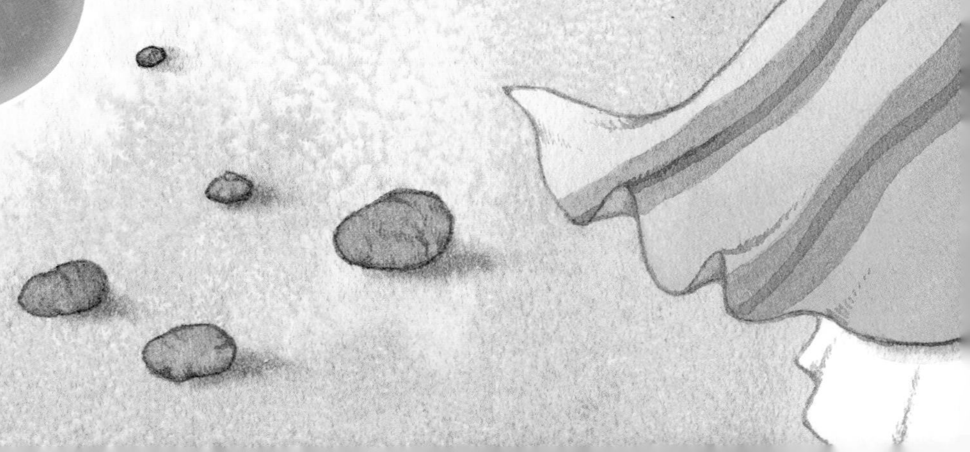

"Each morning some bread will come at first light.
The bread, it is manna, collect it six nights.
The sixth day you must get twice what you need.
Take only so much; do not act with greed.

"You're hungry by day and hungry by night.
You will have food before next morning's light.
Our God is still here; he's caring for you.
Always obey the Lord in what you do."

The next morning dawned with dew on the ground.
The people got up and scattered around.
When the dew dried, some thin white flakes appeared.
"It's bread!" they said, and then they all cheered.

Now they ate food, just as Moses had said.
God sent from heaven the fresh, tasty bread.
God gives what we need and cares for us, too.
So you can trust God to take care of you.

# Activities

A child delights in the pure silliness that often accompanies rhyming activities. When a child makes up words that aren't really words, but which rhyme, he increases his joy in using language and continues to build mastery. Capture spontaneous opportunities to play rhyming games. For instance, when you have an empty cardboard tube, say a word into one end and ask your child to whisper back a rhyming word. Or when you are watching a child swing, call out "What rhymes with red?" or "What rhymes with toy?" Informal learning times like these contribute to building a language-rich environment.

## Game to **play**

*Help your child complete these riddles with the information in Exodus 16:1-26.*

The flakes people ate rhyme with the name Hannah;
the flakes that fell from the sky were called _____. (manna)

God watched his people so they wouldn't get hurt
as they wandered around, in the hot dry _____. (desert)

A few people hunted for food on day seven;
but as Moses said, nothing fell then from _____. (heaven)

## Song to **sing**

*Sing to the tune of "The Farmer in the Dell."*

God gives us what we need,
God gives us what we need,
We don't need to worry 'cause
God gives us what we need.

## Verse to **say**

"God can bless you with everything you need." *2 Corinthians 9:8, CEV*

## Prayer to **pray**

Dear God, thank you for giving me what I need. Amen.

# The Silky Red Rope

**BIBLE TRUTH**
God protects us.

**LEARNING FUN**
Identifying textures

**SCRIPTURE REFERENCE**
Joshua 2:1-21

**MEMORY VERSE**
"The Lord protects his people, and they can come to him in times of trouble."
*Psalm 37:39, CEV*

Before you read the story, ask your child to pay special attention to the "texture" words, such as bumpy or sharp, and try to picture them as you read.

The two spies crouched low in the shadows. One of the men groaned as he knelt to rest on sharp rocks. But the spies stopped only a little while, and soon they stumbled across the bumpy stones to Rahab's home.

Motioning for the men to come inside, Rahab whispered, "You can't stay here. The king's soldiers will find you."

"Then hide us," said one spy. "We are on a mission for Joshua, the leader of God's people."

"Yes, hide us," encouraged the other man. "Can't we huddle under that rough cloth in the corner? Or behind that big table?"

Shaking her head, Rahab said, "No. The soldiers would find you." She motioned for the spies to follow her up the uneven steps to the roof. Rahab pushed aside plant stalks that had been laid out to dry. The plants crunched as the men hid underneath.

The soldiers came in looking for the spies, but decided to search near the city gate instead. Rahab watched the soldiers leave, then carried a long, silky rope to the roof. Moving aside the dry stalks, Rahab uncovered the spies.

"I know God has given this land to your people," she said. "When you come for this land, be as kind to me as I have been to you this night." The spies agreed. Then Rahab gave them the smooth rope.

"My house is built into the city wall. Slide down this rope and you will land outside," she said. "Then stay behind prickly plants in the hills for three days until the soldiers stop searching for you."

Grateful, the spies prepared to lower themselves over the stony wall. Pausing briefly, one of the men said, "After we have escaped, hang up this silky red rope. That will remind our men to protect you."

The spies then escaped into the night. Rahab tied the slippery red rope to the window, and she remained safe.

# Activities

Informal teaching with positive statements helps draw the line between scaring a child and prioritizing safety. For example, when strapping a child into a car seat you might say, "When we hear the buckle 'click,' that means you'll stay in your seat if the car stops suddenly." This emphasizes the aspect of your trust relationship, which reflects, "I'm doing my best to keep you safe." You can also emphasize that God keeps us safe by saying something such as "Aren't you glad God gives us seat belts to keep us safe?" A child who knows his parents are working to keep him safe will believe more readily that God keeps him safe, too.

## Questions to **ask**

What kinds of things protect you? *If your child can't think of anything, suggest things such as seat belts, sunscreen, helmets, knee pads, and bug spray.*

How does God protect you? *Take this opportunity to share with your child ways you know that God has protected you, your child, or someone you know.*

## Game to play

*Each time you and your child play this game, your child will probably insert different words. For example, your child might initially say, "soft as a feather." In later readings, your child might say "soft as the baby's blanket" or "soft as my skin after a bath." This will reflect your child's growing vocabulary and understanding of specific textures.*

Fill in the blanks:

soft as a _____
sticky like a _____
sharp as a _____
light as a _____
rough like a _____
fluffy as a _____
sparkly as a _____
fuzzy like a _____
slick as a _____
spongy like a _____
shaggy as a _____

## Verse to say

"The Lord protects his people, and they can come to him in times of trouble."
*Psalm 37:39, CEV*

## Prayer to pray

Dear God, when I worry about things that might happen, help me remember you will always be with me and protect me. Amen.

# God Wins the Battle

**BIBLE TRUTH**
Praise God because he does incredible things.

**LEARNING FUN**
Qualities of movement: fast and slow

**SCRIPTURE REFERENCE**
Judges 4

**MEMORY VERSE**
"I will sing to the Lord, I will sing; I will make music to the Lord, the God of Israel." *Judges 5:3, NIV*

**H**urry, Barak, **hurry,**" said a messenger. "Deborah wants to see you."

Barak **rushed** to meet God's prophet. He knew just where to find her: Deborah always sat under her palm tree. Breathless from **running**, Barak said, "What do you want?"

"God wants you to gather an army against the evil Sisera," Deborah told Barak. "God will help you win at Mount Tabor."

"Me? Against the evil Sisera?" asked Barak, **slowly** backing away. "Well, if you go with me, I will go. If you don't go, I won't go."

Deborah agreed, "I will go with you."

Barak walked away **slowly**. "How can we win against Sisera?" Barak wondered. He **dragged** his feet. He was not looking forward to this. Deborah **hurried** to Mount Tabor. Barak gathered his troops.

When Sisera heard that Barak's soldiers were waiting to fight him at the mountain, he **quickly** rounded up 900 chariots. Sisera was ready for anything.

Barak and his troops waited patiently. Barak moved **slowly**. He was not eager to meet Sisera.

Finally Deborah said, "The Lord has gone before you. Today is the day. **Hurry**, Barak, **hurry**. Go down the mountain."

As Barak's troops **raced** down Mount Tabor, God confused Sisera. The evil leader, his chariot drivers, and his whole army were mixed up. Sisera and all his soldiers were wiped out.

Barak **raced** back to Deborah. "We won!" Barak shouted.

"God won the battle for us," Deborah reminded him. "Let's give him our praise and thanks."

# Activities

## To the parent

When talking about the qualities of movement (fast and slow) with a child, we naturally think of racing to get an ice cream cone or dragging to bed. But you can also point out the qualities of movement in inanimate objects. For example, if you and a child lie down on your backs and look up at the sky, can you see clouds move? Leaves move? Flags flutter? How does the movement change when the wind starts to blow? Or, when a child stomps snow off boots, you might observe, "That makes the snow fall off quickly."

## Game to play

*Ask your child to play this fast/slow game with you.*

Jump fast.
Smile slow.
Clap fast.
Walk backwards slow.
Giggle fast.
Stomp fast.
Wiggle your ears slow.
Blink fast.
Hug me fast.

## Song to **sing**

*Deborah and Barak sang praises to God. You can, too! Sing "Praise Him, Praise Him" together.*

Praise him, praise him,
Praise him in the morning,
Praise him in the noontime.
Praise him, praise him,
Praise him when the sun goes down.

## Verse to **say**

"I will sing to the Lord, I will sing; I will make music to the Lord, the God of Israel." *Judges 5:3, NIV*

## Prayer to **pray**

Dear God, you do so many incredible things. I want to especially praise you for _____. Amen.

# From Eighth to First

**BIBLE TRUTH**
God has a plan for us.

**LEARNING FUN**
Ordinals: first through eighth

**SCRIPTURE REFERENCE**
1 Samuel 16:1-13

**MEMORY VERSE**
"'I know the plans I have for you,' declares the Lord."
*Jeremiah 29:11, NIV*

Jesse's sons lined up for Samuel. God had told Samuel one of these boys would be the next king, but who would it be? Samuel knew God would tell him when he saw the son God planned to make the next king.

The **first** son was tall and handsome, but this wasn't the one God had planned to be king. Samuel shook his head no.

The **second** son had slicked down his hair, but this wasn't the one God had planned to be king. Samuel shook his head no.

The **third** son had a long, scruffy beard, but this wasn't the one God had planned to be king. Samuel shook his head no.

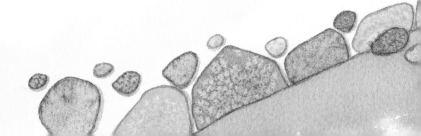

The **fourth** son wore sandals so new that they creaked, but this wasn't the one God had planned to be king. Samuel shook his head no.

The **fifth** son wore a fine, thick coat, but this wasn't the one God had planned to be king. Samuel shook his head no.

The **sixth** son had hair so shiny it glistened, but this wasn't the one God had planned to be king. Samuel shook his head no.

The **seventh** son wore a soft, fluffy cloak, but this wasn't the one God had planned to be king. Samuel shook his head no.

Then Samuel asked, "Where is your **eighth** son?"

"David is my youngest," Jesse answered. "He is watching the sheep."

Samuel said, "I must see all eight boys. Please bring David to me."

Soon the youngest son ran in from the fields. David wore the scruffy clothing of a shepherd. He smelled like he had slept in his clothes, but Samuel smiled. This was the one God had planned to be king. Samuel nodded yes.

"Your **eighth** son is the one God has chosen," Samuel said. And the shepherd boy became the next king.

# Activities

Children love sequential stories because they know what will come next. Even the mental anticipation of third, fourth, and fifth in this lesson gives a comforting sense of order. This is the same underlying reason many children choose to hear the same story repeated over and over: they know exactly what happens.

## Game to **play**

*This game will help your child understand the concept of ordinals. Ask your child to fill in the blanks with the rhyming word.*

This happened first:
First I was a baby so in my crib I'd lie,
and if I got fussy I'd get so mad I'd _____. (cry)

This happened second:
Next I was a toddler; that's when I learned to walk.
I'd do so many things; I even learned to _____. (talk)

This happened third:
Now that I am older and growing all the time
I run and play and hop; I even make words _____. (rhyme)

This will happen fourth:
Next year I'll be taller and even smarter, too.
Just wait to hear the words: "I will read to _____." (you)

## Questions to ask

*David was a shepherd before God chose him to be king. Flocks of sheep needed to be watched all the time, because sheep were very important animals. Sheep gave food to eat and wool for making clothes and tents. Talk about sheep with your child by answering these questions:*

Which have you seen more often, a sheep or a shepherd?
A sheep or a squirrel? A sheep or a lamb?
Would a sheep make a good pet? Why or why not?
Which would weigh more: a sheep before or after shearing?

## Verse to say

"'I know the plans I have for you,' declares the Lord." *Jeremiah 29:11, NIV*

## Prayer to pray

Dear God, help me trust that you know what is best, and that you have a plan for me. Amen.

# The Tall and the Small

**BIBLE TRUTH**
God is stronger than anyone or anything.

**LEARNING FUN**
Opposites

**SCRIPTURE REFERENCE**
1 Samuel 17:1-50

**MEMORY VERSE**
"O Lord God Almighty, who is like you? You are mighty, O Lord." *Psalm 89:8, NIV*

The *big* voice boomed across the battlefield, "Who will come and fight me?"

In a *small* voice David whispered to his brother, a soldier, "Who said that?"

His brother whispered, "That's Goliath, the giant. Every *morning*, he teases us like that. And then he does the same thing every *evening*."

David looked across the battlefield at the very *big older* man. David was a very *small younger* man.

But he said, "Goliath is making fun of us and God. I will fight Goliath. I will show everyone that God is stronger than anyone or anything."

David's brother said, "You are small. Goliath is big. You cannot fight Goliath."

But David said, "I will not be alone. God will be with me."

David told King Saul that he would fight Goliath. So King Saul helped David put on the king's large, heavy armor and helmet. But David could not move. He took off the armor and picked up his small, light slingshot.

Next, King Saul helped David lift the king's large, heavy shield. But David could not carry it. Instead, he picked up his small, light bag with a few stones.

Finally, King Saul gave David the king's large, heavy sword, but David could not swing it. So David picked up his small, light shepherd's stick.

Goliath marched out to the battlefield. He looked very big. David marched out to the battlefield. David looked very small, but he said boldly, "The true God does not need swords and spears to save his people. God always wins his battles, and today he will defeat you, because he is stronger than anyone or anything."

Angrily, Goliath stomped forward. David put a rock into his slingshot and swung the sling around. The rock whizzed through the air and cracked Goliath on the forehead. Goliath fell to the ground. David stood tall, for he had shown everyone that God was stronger than a giant.

# Activities

Informal word play, as suggested in the activity below, is one of the easiest ways to teach a child about contrast. A child is exposed to opposites through everyday activities, so with a minimum of adult assistance, he can understand the concept. As with any early childhood activity, nurturing joy in learning is at least as important as developing the skill.

## Game to **play**

*What's the opposite? Fill in the blanks:*

fat - thin
out - _____(in)

hot - cold
open - _____(fold)

dark - light
day - _____(night)

down - up
plate - _____(cup)

## Rhyme to *say*

When David was a little boy
keeping track of sheep,
I wonder if he dreamed at night
when he fell asleep.

I wonder if young David knew
that he alone would stand
upon the battlefield so soon,
a slingshot in his hand.

Now David knew that God was strong;
a mighty God was he.
His God would watch and comfort him
wherever he would be.

## Verse to *say*

"O Lord God Almighty, who is like you? You are mighty, O Lord."
*Psalm 89:8, NIV*

## Prayer to **pray**

Dear God, even when I have problems, help me remember that you will help me, because you are bigger and stronger than my problems. Amen.

# The Mean Fool

**BIBLE TRUTH**
We should be kind to
each other.

**LEARNING FUN**
We eat a variety of foods

**SCRIPTURE REFERENCE**
1 Samuel 25:2-42

**MEMORY VERSE**
"Do all you can for everyone
who deserves your help."
Proverbs 3:27, CEV

David and his friends were wonderful neighbors. They were friendly to others. They helped farmers find lost animals. They even helped protect the flocks of their rich neighbor, Nabal, who owned three thousand sheep and a thousand goats.

One day, when David and his friends couldn't find food, David asked Nabal to share some food. But Nabal said no.

When Nabal's wife, Abigail, heard this, she shook her head and said, "Nabal is a fool." Abigail knew her husband was a mean bully.

Abigail quickly loaded a huge feast onto donkeys. She gathered a sack of grain, the meat from five sheep, a hundred handfuls of raisins, two hundred loaves of bread, and two hundred handfuls of dried figs.

Then Abigail led the servants and the feast onto the hill path. Abigail couldn't see or hear David and his men, but they were coming around the other side of the hill.

David and his men had been talking about Nabal's selfishness. They even made up jokes about Nabal's name, which meant fool.

As David and his men roared with laughter, they rode around the side of the hill. Abigail and her servants came around the other side. The two groups met on the hill path. Quickly, Abigail slid off her donkey and knelt at David's feet.

"Please don't pay attention to my husband. Nabal's name means fool, and you know that's exactly what he is," Abigail said. "Please accept this food."

David looked at the kind woman who knelt at his feet. Graciously, he accepted her gifts.

"God will make you ruler over all his people," Abigail said to David. "When that happens, please remember me."

Nabal was punished for his foolishness, but David remembered Abigail's kindness.

# Activities

Most children like to make choices. Sampling a variety of foods maximizes their growing ability to make decisions and increases the potential of a balanced diet. However, "food jags," or times when a child prefers a very limited number of foods (perhaps even the same item for breakfast, lunch, and supper!), are also common during the early childhood years. Although these "jags" can last for weeks or months, children eventually expand their diets and return to healthier eating patterns.

## Game to **play**

*Guess the food. Which foods are these?*

Bunnies love me. They go munch munch.
I am orange and I come in a _____. (bunch – carrot)

I start out green, but redden as I grow.
You like me on sandwiches. I'm a _____. (tomato)

I'm red, green, or yellow. I grow on a tree,
I make applesauce; for snacks you love _____. (me – apple)

When my shucks are torn,
I'm underneath! I'm _____. (corn)

I am long and lean.
I'm a green _____. (bean)

## Questions to **ask**

Which foods do we chew and which do we sip?
- candy bar
- lemonade
- hamburger
- hot chocolate
- soup
- potato chips

## Verse to **say**

"Do all you can for everyone who deserves your help." *Proverbs 3:27, CEV*

## Prayer to **pray**

Dear God, when I don't know what to do, help me to remember you, and what you would have me say. Show me how to live each day. Amen.

# Hammerin' Hiram

**BIBLE TRUTH**
We should praise God.

**LEARNING FUN**
Shapes

**SCRIPTURE REFERENCE**
1 Kings 5–7

**MEMORY VERSE**
"Come to worship [the Lord] with thankful hearts and songs of praise."
*Psalm 95:2, CEV*

Hiram, Hiram, pound away.
Build a church for God today.
Make it big and make it right
so it's pleasing in God's sight.

Columns **round** should stand so tall
in the biggest room of all.
Windows **square** should line a row,
letting in God's light, you know.

Outside columns – **circles** stand,
Hiram, Hiram, lend a hand.
Help the workers bring the wood –
fresh cut cedar smells so good.

Panels of bright bronze stand **square**
with the **circles** under there.
At the top a nine-inch strip
of **rectangles** around the tip.

Hiram, Hiram, add some gold;
then pour bronze into a mold.
Shape some bowls and pans now, too.
Everything should be brand-new.

Hiram hammered day and night.
God's church was a great, great sight.
It took twenty years to build
the temple just as God had willed.

People came to sing and praise.
Songs went on for many days.
People played on trumpets, too.
Singers sang, "God, we praise you."

# Activities

The sequence for learning about shapes is to recognize a shape when asked (the child points to the shape), correctly name the shape, and then spontaneously identify the shape. Circle and square are the first two shapes a child learns, followed by rectangle and then more specialized shapes such as diamond and hexagon. Reinforce shape identification by referring to street signs. For example, when stopped at a railroad crossing you might ask, "What shape is that yellow sign?"

## Game to **play**

*Look back at the temple illustrations and help your child identify these shapes in the temple:*
- circles
- squares
- rectangles

## Song to **sing**

*Sing "Praise Him, Praise Him" together.*

Praise him, praise him, all you little children;
God is love, God is love.
Praise him, praise him, all you little children;
God is love, God is love.

Love him, love him all you little children.
Thank him, thank him, all you little children.

## Verse to **say**

"Come to worship [the Lord] with thankful hearts and songs of praise."
*Psalm 95:2, CEV*

## Prayer to **pray**

Dear God, I praise you for all the wonderful things that you do. Thank you for
your house where we can go to learn about you and sing songs to you. Amen.

# The Queen Comes to Visit

**BIBLE TRUTH**
God gives us wisdom.

**LEARNING FUN**
True or false

**SCRIPTURE REFERENCE**
1 Kings 10:1-13

**MEMORY VERSE**
"If any of you need wisdom, you should ask God, and it will be given to you."
*James 1:5, CEV*

God made King Solomon the wisest man in the world. Solomon wrote three thousand wise sayings. He wrote more than one thousand songs. People everywhere heard about his wisdom.

God also made King Solomon the richest man in the world. King Solomon's throne was made of ivory and covered with gold. His ships brought gold and silver, as well as monkeys and peacocks.

King Solomon was so wise and so rich that he was famous all over the world. Even the Queen of Sheba had heard about Solomon's greatness. Each time people came to visit the Queen of Sheba, she would ask, "Who is the wisest man in the world?" And every person answered, "King Solomon."

One day, the queen asked to herself, "Is it *true* or *false*? Is Solomon really the wisest and richest man in the world?"

The queen wanted to find out for herself. So she loaded her camels with gifts for the king. She took gold, jewels, and many rare spices. When she reached King Solomon, the queen started to ask him questions.

The queen asked about all kinds of plants, from large trees to small bushes. King Solomon answered each question correctly.

The queen asked about animals. The queen asked about birds, reptiles, and fish. King Solomon answered every single question correctly. The queen of Sheba was amazed.

The queen was also amazed when she saw King Solomon's palace, the food on his table, his servants in their uniforms, and the way he worshiped God in the beautiful temple.

"Solomon," the queen said, "I had heard about your wisdom and your riches. But I thought it might be *false* until I saw it with my own eyes. Now I know it is *true*. You are the wisest and richest man in the world. God has blessed your people with a king who is wise and will rule fairly and honestly."

# Activities

## To the parent

Your child and the biblical Queen of Sheba are similar in one way: they both like to determine fact from fiction by seeing for themselves. But drawing that line has become complicated for children today. The visual realities that are brought into our homes through media so often mix truth and fantasy that it may be hard to distinguish where reality stops and imagination begins. A child can be reminded that the Bible lessons in this book are real by prefacing the stories with the words, "This is what really happened long ago."

## Questions to ask

What does it mean to make wise choices?

Would you rather be wise or rich?

How much money does it take to be rich?

Where does wisdom come from?

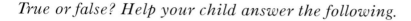

# Game to play

*True or false? Help your child answer the following.*

True or false: Planes fly.
True or false: Boats fly.

True or false: Dogs meow.
True or false: Dogs bark.

True or false: Babies cry.
True or false: Babies smile.

True or false: Phones ring.
True or false: Phones talk.

True or false: Scissors cut.
True or false: Scissors spill.

True or false: Rain squirts.
True or false: Rain falls.

# Verse to say

"If any of you need wisdom, you should ask God, and it will be given to you."
*James 1:5, CEV*

# Prayer to pray

Dear God, thank you for helping me be wise, for opening up my heart and eyes, for helping me to learn about you I give you thanks in all I do. Amen.

# Birds Bring Food

**BIBLE TRUTH**
We can trust God.

**LEARNING FUN**
Ordinals: first through fourth

**SCRIPTURE REFERENCE**
1 Kings 17:1-6

**MEMORY VERSE**
"Trust the Lord with all your heart." *Proverbs 3:5, ICB*

This happened first:

The (king) and (queen) built statues

all over the country. (people)

prayed to the statues.

This happened second:

God's servant (Elijah) went to

visit the (king) and (queen).

 (Elijah) told them, "You have

disobeyed God. Your (people)

are praying to statues.

God will punish you and the .
people

There will be no . Not a single drop
rain

of  will fall. Then you will see that
rain

God is the one true God."

This happened third:

 went away from the  and .
Elijah                                        king         queen

 went far away from the
Elijah                                      people

praying to the statues. God told  to
Elijah

hide by a .
brook

This happened fourth:

Just as God said, no  fell.
rain

 drank water from the .
Elijah                                           brook

He had 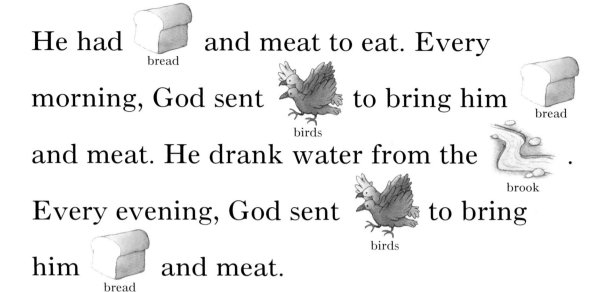 and meat to eat. Every morning, God sent 🐦 *birds* to bring him 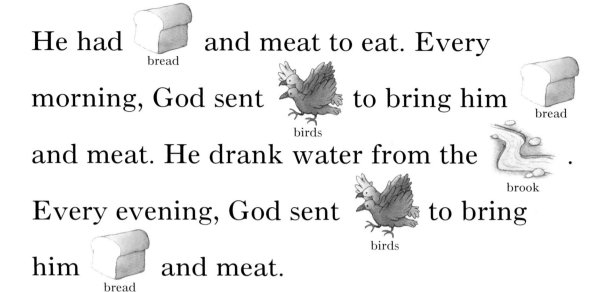 *bread* and meat. He drank water from the 〰️ *brook* . Every evening, God sent 🐦 *birds* to bring him 🍞 *bread* and meat.

🐑 *Elijah* trusted God, and God took good care of 🐑 *Elijah* .

# Activities

## To the parent

Trust begins early in life, when an infant's needs are consistently met. Even though a young child cannot define trust, he learns it means believing that people will do what they say. A child counts on you to catch him at the bottom of the slide; a child believes that you will buy that ice cream cone you promised; a child knows that you will comfort him during a storm. In early childhood, children learn to trust adults. The scenario flips as children grow up, as gradually adults learn to trust children.

## Game to play

*Ask your child to put the following in order of first, second, third, and fourth. For some there may be only one right answer, but others could work several ways.*

Put on sunscreen. Jump into the pool. Take off sandals. Put on a swimsuit.

Wash dirty dishes. Set the table. Eat lunch. Make lunch.

Put on pajamas. Go to sleep. Brush your teeth. Pray.

Tear open a present. Open a card. Send a thank-you note. Take off the ribbon.

Say "Thank you." Wash your hands. Say "Please." Eat an ice cream cone.

## Song to Sing

*Sing "God Is So Good" together.*

God is so good,
God is so good,
God is so good,
He's so good to me.

I trust him so,
I trust him so,
I trust him so,
He's so good to me.

## Verse to Say

"Trust the Lord with all your heart." *Proverbs 3:5, ICB*

## Prayer to Pray

Dear God, I am so glad I can trust you! Amen.

# Race Through the Rain

**BIBLE TRUTH**
God is all-powerful.

**LEARNING FUN**
Observing weather

**SCRIPTURE REFERENCE**
1 Kings 18:41-46

**MEMORY VERSE**
"Tell about God's power!
He is honored in Israel, and
he rules the skies."
*Psalm 68:34, CEV*

One beautiful sunny day, Elijah told his servant, "Soon it will rain."

His servant was amazed. The sky was blue. The sun was bright. When the servant didn't even see a cloud in the sky, Elijah said, "Go and look toward the sea."

The servant went to look, but didn't see anything unusual. The sky was blue. The sun was bright.

Elijah told him to go back and look again.

The servant went to look again, but nothing had changed. The sky was blue. The sun was bright.

Again and again the servant went back to look at the sea. Finally, the seventh time, the servant said, "I see only one small cloud." The sky was still blue and the sun was still bright.

Yet Elijah said to his servant, "Tell King Ahab to get his chariot ready and start for home. Otherwise, he will get caught in the rain."

King Ahab had caused a lot of trouble for Elijah. The king didn't believe in the one true God. The king didn't believe what Elijah, God's servant, said either.

A few minutes later, big, dark clouds gathered in the sky. A strong wind started to blow. Thunder rumbled. A few large drops plopped to the ground, then the rain began to pour down.

Elijah wrapped his coat around him, and the Lord gave him strength to run all the way back to the city.

Much later, King Ahab returned in his chariot. He was soaking wet.

# Activities

Watching the weather is one of the first ways a child learns the science-related skills of observing and recording information. You might designate one window as the "weather window." Then around the same time each day (breakfast or lunch works well) observe the weather with your child. A child can draw a simple symbol (cloud, sun, raindrop) or representative color (gray for cloudy, blue for rainy, yellow for sunny) in the daily squares on the family calendar. Observations are most interesting during the transitional months of spring and fall, when a child will see a variety of weather conditions.

## Questions to **ask**

What does a thermometer measure?

When you wake up in the morning, how do you find out about the day's weather?

What kind of weather do you like best?

What type of weather would you be having if you said:
• Let's go fly a kite.
• These boots are too small.
• I'll take an umbrella.
• Where's my shovel?
• Mom, the electricity went out.
• I need more suntan lotion.

## Song to **Sing**

*Sing to the tune of "Old MacDonald Had a Farm."*

Our God is all-powerful, and I will tell you so.
Our God is all-powerful, and I will tell you so.
He's big and strong,
so all day long
I'll tell it here, I'll tell it there, I will tell it everywhere.
Our God is all-powerful, and I will tell you so.

## Verse to **say**

"Tell about God's power! He is honored in Israel, and he rules the skies."
*Psalm 68:34, CEV*

## Prayer to **pray**

Dear God, when skies are sunny or rain starts to fall, you are the one Lord who watches us all. Amen.

# A Very Special Jar

**BIBLE TRUTH**
God takes care of us.

**LEARNING FUN**
Size: small, medium, and large

**SCRIPTURE REFERENCE**
2 Kings 4:1-7

**MEMORY VERSE**
"God cares for you."
1 Peter 5:7, CEV

As you read this story, encourage your child to use his hands to show small, medium, and large at the appropriate times.

Since your father died, we haven't had money to pay our bills," a mother said sadly to her sons. "If I do not pay, you boys will be taken away."

"Father always said God would take care of us," the older son reminded his mother. "God will take care of us now."

God's servant Elisha heard about their problem. He asked, "Tell me, what do you have in the house?"

The woman said, "I only have one jar of oil."

Elisha said to the boys, "Go to your neighbors. Borrow all the empty jars you can find."

Eager to help, the boys started knocking on doors. Soon, the older son returned with a small jar. The younger son returned with a medium-sized jar. Then the older son struggled through the door with a large jar. But Elisha said, "Don't stop now. Borrow jars from everyone."

The boys ran up and down the streets. Soon small jars, medium-sized jars, and large jars were stacked in every room of their house. Finally, Elisha said, "Shut the door. Now pour your oil into the jars."

The woman carefully took her single jar of oil. She poured the oil slowly into a small jar. There was still oil in her jar. Then she poured oil into a medium-sized jar. There was still oil in her jar. Next she poured oil into a large jar. But she still had oil in her jar.

Again the boys watched their mother pour oil into a small jar, then a medium-sized jar, then a large jar. Again and again they filled more jars!

"Please bring me another small jar," she said.

"There isn't one," said the older boy.

"Please bring me another medium-sized jar," she said.

"There isn't one," said the younger boy. "Mother, there isn't even a large jar left to fill. All the small jars, medium-sized jars, and large jars are full of oil."

The woman looked into her jar. It was completely empty.

Elisha looked at the crowded rooms and said, "Sell the oil in the jars. Then you will have money to pay your bills and live in your house."

Gratefully, the woman thanked Elisha. She sold the oil, paid the bills, and saved the rest of the money. The boys returned all the small jars, medium-sized jars, and large jars. And they all knew that God had taken care of them.

# Activities

## To the **parent**

Small, medium, and large: all size is relative. To gain a child's perspective of size, crawl into a room. This is the level at which a young child views the world. As you sit on the floor and look at a sea of chair legs, labels glued underneath furniture, and perhaps a few dust bunnies, it's easy to understand why children respond so positively when adults kneel to meet them at their eye level.

## Game to **play**

*Ask your child to list the following items in order by size from smallest to largest.*

A kitten, an ant, an elephant

A shoe, a coat, a glove

A car, an airplane, a bike

A Bible, a church, a chair

## Song to **sing**

*Sing to the tune of "Twinkle, Twinkle, Little Star."*

God will take good care of you—
keep you safe the whole day through.
When you work and when you play,
as you go throughout your day,
God will take good care of you.
He'll keep you safe the whole day through.

## Verse to **say**

"God cares for you." *1 Peter 5:7, CEV*

## Prayer to **pray**

Dear God, help me remember that you will take care of me. Amen.

# Muddy Water

**BIBLE TRUTH**
We should obey people who tell us to do what is right.

**LEARNING FUN**
Visual recognition: 1–7

**SCRIPTURE REFERENCE**
2 Kings 5:1-14

**MEMORY VERSE**
"The Lord your God is the only true God. . . . Obey his commands."
*Deuteronomy 7:9, CEV*

Naaman, the brave general of the army, was very sick. His skin was covered with sores. He had sores on his ears. He had sores under his fingernails. He had sores everywhere. One day Naaman counted his sores: He had **7** sores just on his elbow!

When Elisha, one of God's helpers, heard about the sickness, Elisha invited Naaman to come to him.

Elisha's messenger told Naaman, "Wash yourself **7** times in the Jordan River. Then you will be cured."

Naaman grumbled. He would get all dirty. The Jordan river was muddy. Then Naaman's servant suggested, "It sounds very simple, and you are very sick. Why don't you try it? Just dip **7** times in the river."

Still grumbling, Naaman went to the muddy river. Sinking in the oozing brown mud, Naaman slowly waded into the water. **1, 2, 3** times he dipped down into the water. Each time Naaman came up, his skin was still covered with sores. **4, 5, 6** times he dipped down into the water. His skin was still covered with sores.

Once again Naaman dipped into the muddy water. When he came up, he was muddy, but the sores were gone. The sores were entirely gone! He had dipped into the water **7** times and now he was healed, just as God's helper had promised.

# Activities

Obedience begins very simply when a child puts away his toys and makes his bed. As a child grows, he learns, respects, and gradually embraces the rules, which become personal guidelines for behavior. A child develops a great deal of security within boundaries that are consistent, because he knows his limits. We nurture obedience by clearly communicating necessary rules, enforcing them in loving and responsive ways, and affirming a child who follows the rules.

## Game to **play**

How many numerals can you find? Walk around the house with your child. Look up, down, and all around. Encourage your child to find as many numerals as he can. He might find numerals on a phone, on cards in a wallet, on a clock, stove, dog tag, or calendar.

## Song to Sing

*Sing to the tune of "Are You Sleeping?"*

You are so sick,
you are so sick,
army man,
army man.
God will heal you soon now.
Listen to his helper,
army man,
army man.

You'll feel better,
you'll feel better,
army man,
army man.
Dip into the water,
muddy, muddy water,
seven times,
seven times.

God has healed you,
God has healed you.
God is good,
God is good.
Listen to God's helpers,
and obey his teaching.
He loves you.
He loves you.

## Verse to Say

"The Lord your God is the only true God. So love him and obey his commands."
*Deuteronomy 7:9, CEV*

## Prayer to pray

Dear God, sometimes I don't want to obey. Sometimes I even grumble and whine. Help me obey people who teach me to do the right things. Amen.

# The Scroll

**BIBLE TRUTH**
We should listen to God's Word.

**LEARNING FUN**
Three-dimensional form: cylinder

**SCRIPTURE REFERENCE**
Jeremiah 36

**MEMORY VERSE**
"The word of the Lord stands forever."
1 Peter 1:25, NIV

Explain to your child that long ago, people did not have books. Instead, they wrote on papyrus plant stalks. Long stalks were laid side by side, then pounded together. Many strips or columns were then rolled up to form a scroll.

Unroll the scroll, write God's words, and people will hear his truth," Jeremiah told his helper, Baruch.

Every day, Baruch would write what God told Jeremiah. And every day the scroll grew longer. When they rolled up the scroll, it was a cylinder.

"Unroll the scroll, write God's words, and people will hear his truth."

Every day, Baruch wrote what God told Jeremiah. And every day, the scroll grew longer. The cylinder grew bigger and bigger. Finally, the men were finished.

Baruch carried the cylinder scroll to the temple. He prayed, "Dear God, I will unroll your scroll and read your words, so people will hear your truth."

At the temple, a crowd gathered around Baruch. The palace officers had even heard about the scroll. They said, "Read it to us."

Again Baruch prayed, "Dear God, I will unroll your scroll and read your words, so people will hear your truth."

Once again, a crowd gathered. The palace officers told the king about the scroll. At the palace, the king said to his helper, "Get that scroll and read it to me."

Baruch gave the scroll to the king's helper. But as the king listened to the man read, he became furious.

The king did not want to hear God's words. After each part of the scroll was read, the king ripped off that section. Then he threw the piece of scroll into the blazing fireplace. This happened again and again, until there was nothing left of the cylinder. The king burned up every piece of the scroll.

Baruch returned to Jeremiah. Baruch told how he unrolled the scroll and read God's words. Then he told how the king ripped apart the scroll and burned it, piece by piece.

Although Jeremiah was very sad to hear what happened, he took a new scroll. Jeremiah told Baruch to begin again. He said, "Unroll a scroll, write God's words, so people can hear his truth." Many years later, other people unrolled the scroll, read God's words, and heard his truth.

# Activities

## To the **parent**

A cylinder, as highlighted in this story, is one of the first three-dimensional shapes a child discovers. A child may roll a piece of paper to make a cylinder, use a cardboard tube as a megaphone, or crawl through a playground tunnel. These are natural ways to learn about this geometric shape. During everyday activities, point out other geometric shapes, including cubes (square box or block), cones (ice cream cone), and spheres (baseball or tennis ball).

## Game to **play**

Have a "Cylinder Hunt." Time yourself and your child for three minutes and see how many cylinders each of you can find in your house. Then talk about all the different things cylinders are used for.

## Song to **sing**

*Sing "The B-I-B-L-E" together.*

The B-I-B-L-E, Yes, that's the book for me!
I stand alone on the Word of God:
The B-I-B-L-E!

## Verse to **say**

"The word of the Lord stands forever." *1 Peter 1:25, NIV*

## Prayer to **pray**

Dear God, help me learn the lessons you teach in the Bible. Amen.

# The Push and Pull Rescue

**BIBLE TRUTH**
God promises
to help us.

**LEARNING FUN**
Opposites: push and pull

**SCRIPTURE REFERENCE**
Jeremiah 38:1-13

**MEMORY VERSE**
"We depend on you, Lord, to help and protect us."
*Psalm 33:20, CEV*

For many months, Jeremiah had preached to the people about God. He encouraged the people to be sorry for their sins. Jeremiah reminded them about the one true God, but his message wasn't popular. Finally, he told the people that their city would be destroyed. So some of the city leaders tried to get rid of Jeremiah by tossing him into an empty well.

Down in the bottom of the hole, mud oozed between Jeremiah's toes. Jeremiah tried to stand in the slime, but he slid sideways, banging against the well wall.

Jeremiah tried to breathe deeply, but the smells clogged his nose.

Trying to keep warm, he shivered as he rubbed his hands together.

A man named Ebedmelech was shocked when he heard about what happened to Jeremiah. When Ebedmelech told the king, the king said, "Take 30 of my soldiers and pull Jeremiah out before he dies."

Ebedmelech found rags and a long rope. Then he and the soldiers hurried to find the well.

Ebedmelech called down into the pit, "Jeremiah?" But only the name "Jeremiah" echoed back. Calling even louder Ebedmelech yelled, "Jeremiah?" Still, there wasn't a sound.

Hoping Jeremiah was still alive, Ebedmelech called into the darkness, "Jeremiah, we are throwing down some old rags. Put the cloths under your armpits so the rope will not burn your skin. Then we will pull you up."

Deep in the darkness, Jeremiah weakly pushed with his legs, so his body didn't bang against the walls of the well.

Above in the sunlight, the soldiers pulled.

"Push," Ebedmelech encouraged Jeremiah.

"Pull," he directed the soldiers. As they tugged, rope began to coil around their feet.

"Push," Ebedmelech called into the pit

"Pull harder," he directed the soldiers.

Soon, a dark head of matted hair appeared at the top of the pit. Ebedmelech and soldiers reached down to pull Jeremiah out of the well.

Squinting in the light, Jeremiah looked at his rescuers. Hoarsely, he said, "God was faithful. He sent you to help me. Thank you, my friends."

# Activities

Children are exposed to many learning concepts through everyday activities. When an adult also defines one of those concepts, a child can validate in his own mind, "Yes, that's what this means." For example, young children typically experience the physical sensation of "pulling" when opening a door and "pushing" when shutting a door. Look for informal opportunities to highlight the contrast between pulling and pushing, which allow a child to match the physical action with the meaning of the word.

## Questions to **ask**

*Ask your child whether you push or pull the following. Some of them you might both push and pull.*

- A friend on a swing
- A dog on a leash
- An apple on a tree
- A doll in a stroller
- A video game button
- A loose tooth
- A rope in a tug of war

## Song to **sing**

*Sing to the tune of "The Farmer in the Dell."*

I know God will help me,
I know God will help me.
He will help me every day,
I know God will help me.

He'll help me do what's right,
He'll help me do what's right.
He will help me every day,
He'll help me do what's right.

## Verse to **say**

"We depend on you, Lord, to help and protect us." *Psalm 33:20, CEV*

## Prayer to **pray**

Dear God, thank you for sending people who love me like _____ and people who take care of me like _____. Amen.

# The Writing on the Wall

**BIBLE TRUTH**
We should worship only God.

**LEARNING FUN**
Context clues

**SCRIPTURE REFERENCE**
Daniel 5

**MEMORY VERSE**
"Do not worship any god except me."
*Exodus 20:3, CEV*

Eat, drink, and be merry. Let's have a very good time," sang the people.

The king was hosting a wonderful party. He had invited a thousand people. The guests drank out of gold and silver cups. They ate the finest foods. The palace was crowded with people having fun.

They sang, "Eat, drink, and be merry. Let's have a very good time."

But suddenly, everyone was quiet. No one talked. No one moved. No one laughed. There was silence.

Writing appeared on the palace wall. The king turned pale. His knees started shaking. His legs became weak.

"What does the writing on the wall say?" the king asked. His smartest advisors looked at the wall. They could not read the writing.

People at the party stared at the wall. They could not read the writing.

The queen could not read it, either. But she said, "An old man named Daniel, who is said to be very wise, lives in the kingdom. Perhaps he can read the writing on the wall."

When the king called Daniel to the palace, the king promised the old man, "If you can read this writing on the wall, I will give you the finest gifts. You will wear purple robes. You will hang a gold chain around your neck."

But Daniel shook his head.

"I will read the writing on the wall, but you may keep your gifts. The one true God sent this message on the wall.

"Even at this wonderful party, you have praised statues," said Daniel. "Even tonight, you have failed to worship the one true God. You will not like the words that have been written here."

Then Daniel turned to the palace wall. He read the words. He read that the kingdom would end.

After Daniel read the writing on the wall, he was given the finest gifts. He wore purple robes. A gold chain hung around his neck.

And the writing on the wall came true that very night: the king was killed and his kingdom ended.

# Activities

## To the **parent**

What does the word "merry" mean? A child who is asked that question will probably define the word as if it were spelled "marry". But a child who hears, "Eat, drink, and be merry, let's have a very good time," may define the word "merry" as having fun. That's because a child gains word meanings from context clues, or information from other words in the text. This is one of the benefits of reading aloud to a child. His listening vocabulary expands simply by hearing unfamiliar words used in appropriate ways.

## Game to **play**

Use a mirror to read this "writing on the wall."

Only
Worship
God

160

## Questions to a**ſk**

When you hear the words, "Eat, drink, and be merry," what does the word "merry" mean? Why are people "merry" at parties? Is it wrong to be "merry"?

When the story said that the king's legs were weak, how do you think he felt? When have you felt like that?

When the story said, "His smartest advisors looked at the wall. They could not read the writing," what does "advisors" mean? Who gives you advice?

What are "statues"? Why is it wrong to praise them?

## Verse to **ſay**

"Do not worship any god except me." *Exodus 20:3, CEV*

## Prayer to **pray**

Dear God, help me remember that worshiping you is a very important part of my life. Amen.

# No, No, I Won't Go

**BIBLE TRUTH**
God cares for us even
when we disobey him.

**LEARNING FUN**
EQ (emotional intelligence)

**SCRIPTURE REFERENCE**
Jonah 1–3

**MEMORY VERSE**
"When I was in trouble,
Lord, I prayed to you, and
you listened to me."
Jonah 2:2, CEV

Follow the physical instructions italicized in the text
(stomping feet, shaking fist, bowing head). Encourage
your child to do the same.

God said to Jonah, "Go to the big city.
Tell the people about me."

*Jonah stomped his feet.*
*Jonah shook his fist.*
*"No, no. I won't go."*

Jonah thought again about what God
said. Jonah did not want to go to the big
city. He did not want to obey God.

*Jonah stomped his feet.*
*Jonah shook his fist.*
*"No, no. I won't go."*

Instead, Jonah climbed aboard a ship.
Jonah told the sailors he was running
from God.

When the ship sailed into a terrible storm, the sailors became afraid of Jonah and his powerful God. When they tossed Jonah overboard, the storm stopped.

Jonah was swallowed by a big fish. Inside the big fish, Jonah prayed.

*He bowed his head.*
*He closed his eyes.*
*"I am sorry, Lord.*
*When you told me to go to the big city,*
*I stomped my feet.*
*I shook my fist.*
*I said, 'I will not go.'*
*Now I will go."*

When Jonah got out of the fish,
he went to the big city.
He told the people about God,
and they believed
God's message.

# Activities

## To the **parent**

Some Bible lessons trigger strong emotional responses. For example, even though Jonah and the fish is a popular story, a young child might be scared when he thinks of Jonah being tossed overboard or living inside a fish. When your child tells or shows you how he feels, use his emotions to begin a conversation of significance. If, for example, your child says, "I'm scared to think about Jonah inside a fish," avoid saying, "You shouldn't feel scared." Honestly sharing and talking about feelings boosts a child's emotional intelligence.

## Questions to **ask**

*Use these questions to start a conversation about emotions with your child, but don't force your child to talk about things if he isn't comfortable.*

How do you feel when you tell Mommy or Daddy, "No!"?

How do you feel when you tell Mommy or Daddy, "Yes!"?

When is a time that you feel sad?

When is a time that you feel happy?

When is a time that you feel scared?

# Song to **sing**

*Sing to the tune of "Are You Sleeping?"*

Who is caring, who is caring
when I fall, when I fall?
God is always with me.
He will always hear me
when I call, when I call.

Who is caring, who is caring
when I fear, when I fear?
God is always with me.
He will always hear me.
He is near, he is near.

Who is caring, who is caring
when I cheer, shout "Hooray"?
God is always with me.
He will always hear me
every day, every day.

Who is caring, who is caring
as I grow, as I grow?
God is always with me.
He will always hear me.
Don't you know, don't you know?

# Verse to **say**

"When I was in trouble, Lord, I prayed to you, and you listened to me."
*Jonah 2:2, CEV*

# Prayer to **pray**

Dear God, I'm glad you took care of Jonah long ago. I'm glad you take care of
me now. Amen.

# New Testament Stories

# A Good News Story

**BIBLE TRUTH**
God's words are true.

**LEARNING FUN**
Listening for facts

**SCRIPTURE REFERENCE**
Luke 1:5-25, 57-66

**MEMORY VERSE**
"Your word is the truth."
*John 17:17, CEV*

Before you begin to read the story, tell your child to listen carefully because you will ask some specific questions at the end.

Zechariah and Elizabeth loved God. For many years, they had asked God for a child. Zechariah, who was a priest, sometimes even stood in the temple and prayed for a child. But Zechariah and Elizabeth were now very old and they still lived alone.

One day, an angel visited Zechariah while he was praying in the temple. The angel said, "God has heard your prayers. Your wife, Elizabeth, will have a son. You will name him John."

Even though Zechariah and Elizabeth had prayed for a child for many years, Zechariah was confused. He asked the angel, "How will I know this will happen? How can we have a son when Elizabeth and I are so old?"

The angel said, "God sent me to tell you this good news. But since you didn't believe me, you will not be able to speak until your son is born."

Zechariah walked out of the temple. He tried to talk, but he could not say a word. Zechariah could not speak at all, just as the angel said.

Soon Elizabeth became pregnant. She gave birth to a baby boy just as the angel said. Their neighbors and relatives thought they would name the baby after his father, but Elizabeth repeated what the angel had told Zechariah: "His name is John."

Zechariah, who still could not speak, wrote the same words on a tablet. "His name is John."

Immediately, Zechariah could speak. Everything happened just as the angel said.

# Activities

"The 5 W's and an H"—who, what, where, when, why, and how—are the key elements in a well-written news story. A child who listens attentively for these same elements in a Bible story will mentally focus on important facts. Before you begin to read a story, tell your child to listen carefully because you will ask some specific questions at the end. After a story, develop questions which reflect who, what, where, when, why, and how, as shown below.

## Questions to ask

For *what* did Zechariah and Elizabeth pray? (a baby)

*Who* told Zechariah he would have a son? (an angel)

*Where* was Zechariah when he saw the angel? (in the temple)

*Why* did the angel say Zechariah wouldn't be able to talk?
(because he didn't believe the angel)

*How* did Elizabeth and Zechariah know what to name their son?
(The angel told them, "His name is John.")

*When* did Zechariah begin talking again? (after the baby was named)

## Game to play

*God's words are true, but some of the sentences below are not true. Ask your child to nod when you read a true statement and shake his head when you read a false statement.*

Rain falls up from the sky.
Christmas is in the summer.
Socks get washed in the washing machine.
You find jelly beans in a Christmas stocking.
If church is too crowded, people sit on the ceiling.
A cow says "moo."
Grass is purple.
A dog wags his ears.

## Verse to say

"Your word is the truth." *John 17:17, CEV*

## Prayer to pray

Dear God, thank you for giving me people who help me learn about the Bible, people such as _____. Amen.

# The Baby Born in Bethlehem

Ask your child to clap once each time he hears the "b" sound.

**BIBLE TRUTH**
Jesus was born as a baby.

**LEARNING FUN**
Initial consonant sound "b"

**SCRIPTURE REFERENCE**
Luke 2:4-7

**MEMORY VERSE**
"For to us a child is born."
*Isaiah 9:6, NIV*

Beyond the hills and valleys,
beneath the evening sky,
lay the town of Bethlehem.

This night was unlike any other,
for a special baby would be born here.

Back away from the busy streets,
hidden behind an inn,
was a lowly barn.

This place was unlike any other,
for a special baby would be born here.

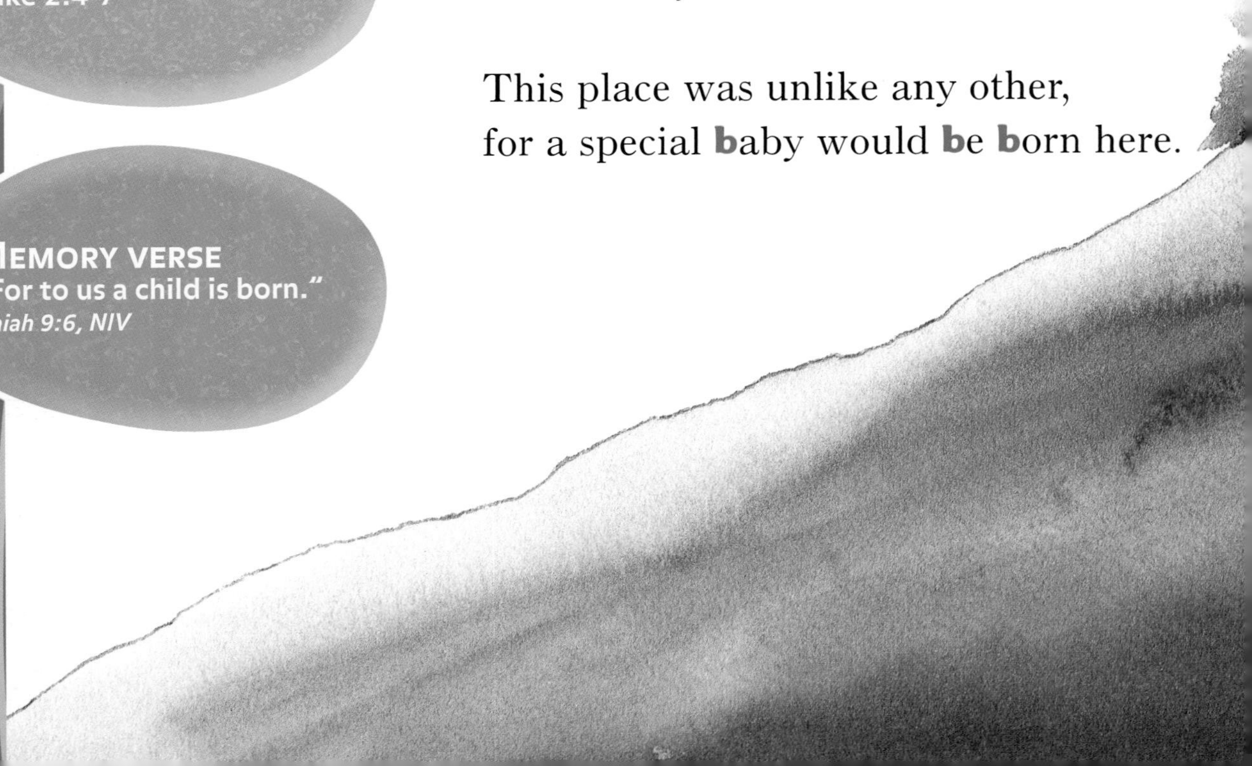

Between the **b**easts and the **b**irds,
tucked into a **b**ed of straw,
Mary gave **b**irth to Jesus.

This child was unlike any other,
for this **b**aby, **b**orn in **B**ethlehem, was the Savior.

# Activities

## To the parent

The "b" sound is one of the first initial consonants a baby vocalizes. Physically, it's an easy sound to make and imitate. You can help your child listen for the initial "b" sound as you see a "bird," "bus," and "bike." As your child begins auditory discrimination (listening for specific sounds) in preparation for reading, focus on these and other words that begin with the pure "b" sound. Later, he will learn to listen for the "b" blends of "bl" (blue) and "br" (brown).

## Game to play

*Help your child identify all the pictures of items that begin with the initial "b" sound.*

## Song to sing

*Sing "O Little Town of Bethlehem" together.*

O little town of Bethlehem,
how still we see thee lie!
Above thy deep and dreamless sleep
the silent stars go by.
Yet in thy dark street shineth
the everlasting Light;
The hopes and fears of all the years
are met in thee tonight.

## Verse to say

"For to us a child is born." *Isaiah 9:6, NIV*

## Prayer to pray

Dear Jesus, I know that Christmas is your birthday. My favorite thing about Christmas is _____. Amen.

*Did you find all the pictures of "b" words? Answers: basket, baby Jesus, bag, beard, bee, bell, bird, box, bucket, bowl, ball, bench, berries, bug, bush.*

# A Shivvery Cold Night

**BIBLE TRUTH**
We should tell the story of Jesus' birth.

**LEARNING FUN**
Temperatures: hot and cold

**SCRIPTURE REFERENCE**
Luke 2:8-20

**MEMORY VERSE**
"Go and preach the good news to everyone in the world." *Mark 16:15, CEV*

**Encourage your child to shake and shiver each time you say the word "shivvery."**

It was **shivvery** cold
chasing a lost sheep through the hills.

It was toasty warm
when the shepherd pulled his cloak
tighter.

It was **shivvery** cold
watching a herd of sheep outside the
town of Bethlehem.

It was toasty warm
around the fire the shepherds
had made.

But the shepherds soon forgot about
keeping warm.

An angel, and then a whole group of
angels, appeared in the sky above.

"Tonight a Savior was born for you," the angel said.
"You will find the Savior in Bethlehem."

It was **shivvery** cold
leaving the warm fire.

It was **shivvery** cold
hurrying over the hills.

It was **shivvery** cold
running through the city streets.

It was toasty warm
when they entered the place where baby Jesus was born.

It was **shivvery** cold
when the shepherds left baby Jesus.

But the shepherds forgot about keeping warm.
They were too excited! They told everyone they saw
the good news that Jesus the Savior was born!

# Activities

## To the **parent**

Children experience dramatic changes in temperature in daily and seasonal activities. After your child learns the basic concepts of hot and cold, help him apply this knowledge. For example, on a hot day, ask, "Would you be cooler playing in the sun or in the shade?" or "Why do you think your ice cream bar melted so fast?" Through this type of informal teaching, your child can learn the meaning of *hot, warm, cool, cold, melt, boil, evaporate,* and *freeze.*

## Questions to **ask**

*Ask your child to hold his arms tightly to his body, as he'd do to keep warm, if the statement you read might happen during cold weather. Ask your child to fan his face if the statement you read might happen in hot weather.*

The ice is frozen on the pond.
Grab your swimsuit!
You will need to wear mittens today.
Please turn on the fan.
Grab a snow shovel.
I'd rather stand in the shade.
The ice cream is melting.
Let's give the snowman a carrot nose.
Smell the pretty flower.
Let's have a picnic.

## Game to play

*Encourage your child to dramatize the story of the shepherds.*
*Italicized words suggest actions your child could do as you read.*

The shepherds *walked* around the hills to guard their sheep that night.
They *walked and walked and walked and walked,* until the sky grew bright.

They *stopped* because above them then some angels soon appeared.
They stood and *trembled, shaking,* for their hearts were filled with fear.

"Fear not," the angel said to them. He spoke from high above.
"The message I bring you this night is full of light and love.

"A Savior has been born to you this night not far from here.
Go now and see him, worship him; there's nothing you must fear."

The shepherds *walked and walked and walked,* until they came to see
the place where baby Jesus lay, now born for you and me.

The story does not stop right here, for shepherds *ran* to say
what happened in that little place on the first Christmas day.

## Verse to say

"Go and preach the good news to everyone in the world." *Mark 16:15, CEV*

## Prayer to pray

Dear Jesus, I know what happened Christmas Day. Help me to know what I
should say so everyone across the earth will hear about your holy birth. Amen.

# Wise Men

**BIBLE TRUTH**
The wise men followed a star.

**LEARNING FUN**
Words that rhyme

**SCRIPTURE REFERENCE**
Matthew 2:1-11

**MEMORY VERSE**
"I often think of the heavens your hands have made, and of the moon and stars you put in place." *Psalm 8:3, CEV*

As you read the story, encourage your child to listen carefully and fill in the blanks with words that rhyme.

A new star shines up in the sky.
Look, over there it is so _____ (high)!
The star's a sign a new king's here.
Let's go and take him gifts of cheer.

"We've watched the star
now twinkling bright
above the sky
on this dark _____ (night).
The star that shines, it is the best.
Let's follow it from east to west."

These wise men rode a long, long way,
through dark of night
and light of _____ (day).
They stopped to ask about the star
that they had followed oh, so far.

But when they asked about the king
whose star they had been following,
The wise men made King Herod mad.
He thought a new king would be _____ (bad).

"A new king born? What's this you say?"
The king was angry on the day
the wise men told about the star
that they had followed oh, so _____ (far).

Now Herod listened with a frown.
He watched the wise men leave the _____ (town).
They left the palace quickly then
and trailed the star to Bethlehem.

And in a house so crude and bare
they found the new king waiting there.
The wise men knelt before the boy
with hearts that overflowed with _____ (joy).

The wise men gave their gifts so rare
to show the king that they did care.

And then they told about the star
that they had followed oh, so _____ (far).

Above the sleepy town that night,
the new star still was burning _____ (bright).
to show to all, from near and far
the Christ child stayed beneath the star.

# Activities

Rhyming simple words, as your child does in this story, often changes into verbal play with silly sounds and nonsense syllables. That's expected during these years when a child experiments to create various words and combinations of sounds. Language is wild and wonderful—that's the message that comes through loud and clear as your child listens to what he is saying. This pure enjoyment of words naturally happens before a child edges closer to learning to read, when he conforms to the rules of language.

## Game to **play**

*Ask your child to complete the sentence with the word that rhymes.*

The sky is dark;
it's clearly night.
But there's a star,
it's shining _____ (bright).

The moon looks big,
the stars look small,
but I know that
God made them _____ (all).

And then when night
is finally done,
I don't see stars,
I see the _____ (sun)!

## Rhyme to say

*Ask your child to wiggle his fingers when you say "twinkling" and put his hands, palms forward and fingers spread, beside his face when you read "shining."*

Star above, now twinkling bright,
shining in the sky at night –
many, many years ago,
God created stars to glow.

Star above, now twinkling bright,
shining in the sky at night,
leading wise men to the bed
where the baby laid his head.

Star above, now twinkling bright,
shining in the sky at night,
showing wise men where to go
to the town that lay below.

Star above, now twinkling bright,
shining in the sky at night –
God made stars, a bright moon, too,
in this world for me and you.

## Verse to say

"I often think of the heavens your hands have made, and of the moon and stars you put in place." *Psalm 8:3, CEV*

## Prayer to pray

Dear God, when I see the stars sparkling at night, I think _____. Thank you for making those twinkling lights. Amen.

# In the Carpenter's Shop

**BIBLE TRUTH**
Jesus grew up
as a child.

**LEARNING FUN**
Simple machines

**SCRIPTURE REFERENCE**
Luke 2:52

**MEMORY VERSE**
"And [Jesus] grew and
became strong . . . and
the grace of God was upon
him." *Luke 2:40, NIV*

Jesus, Jesus,
working away,
helping out
in the shop today.

Jesus, Jesus,
pounding that nail,
hammer hard
so it will not fail.

Jesus, Jesus
follow the rules
while you use
all your father's tools.

Jesus, Jesus,
sawing away,
hold that board;
you will work all day.

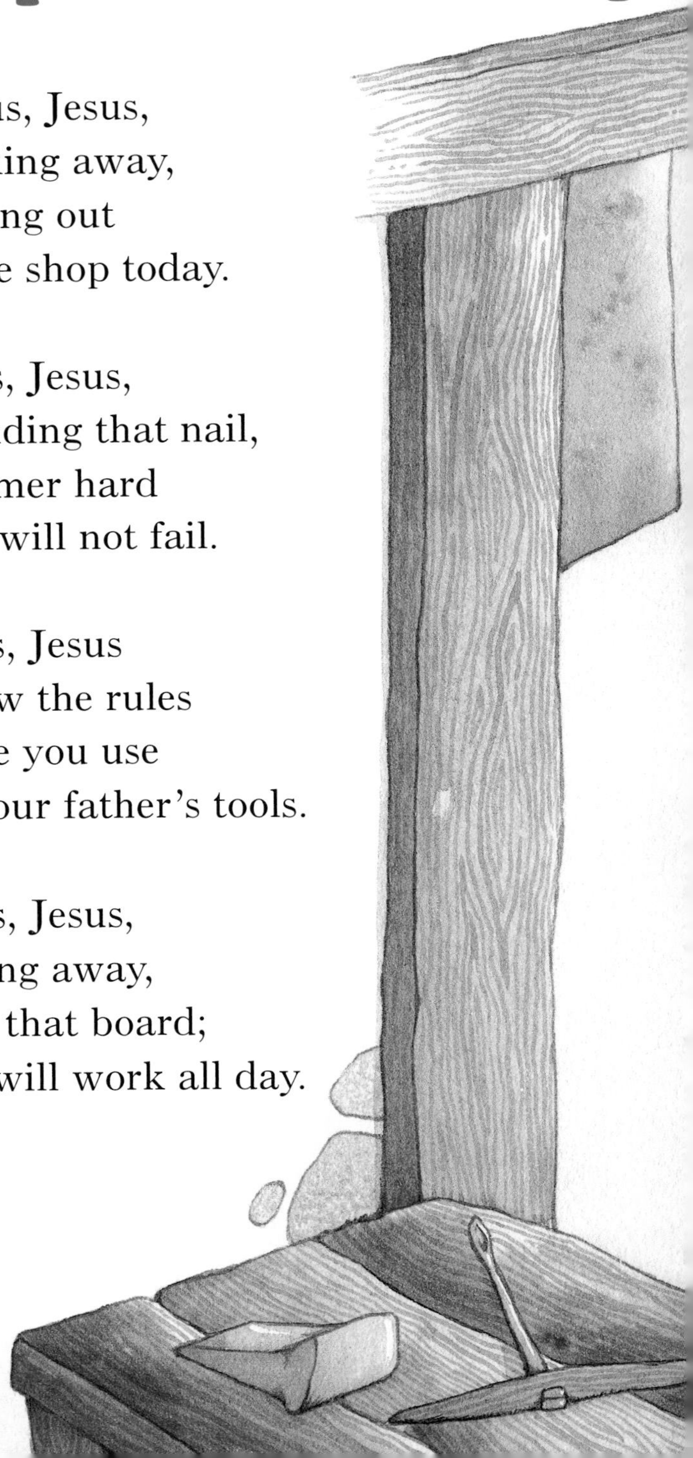

Jesus, Jesus,
helping your dad.
You now make
your father so glad.

Jesus, Jesus,
growing up, too.
God has made
big plans for you!

# Activities

**The six simple machines are the pulley, the lever, the wedge, the wheel and axle, the inclined plane, and the screw. A child sees or uses many of these during normal activities, but learning about these machines does not happen naturally. Take advantage of opportunities to teach your child about simple machines. For example, when your child makes a ramp for miniature cars, you might comment, "You're using an inclined plane to make those vehicles zoom faster." When he holds a fishing rod, you can show how the fish becomes the load for a lever.**

## Game to **play**

*Encourage your child to think about simple machines he uses and sees others use by asking him to fill in the blanks.*

When Daddy wants to chop firewood, he uses an _____ (axe – wedge).

When I want my play cars to go faster, I build a _____ (ramp – inclined plane).

When I pull my toys around, I use my _____ (wagon – wheel and axle).

I go up when my friend goes down on a _____ (seesaw – lever).

A tool to use with a screw is a _____ (screwdriver – screw).

When I watch construction workers lifting heavy beams, I see them use a _____ (crane – pulley).

## To **talk** about

*The Bible tells us about Jesus and other children. Can you find the names of these boys in the Bible?*

The baby boy who was put in a basket: _____ (Exodus 2:10)

The boy who lived in the temple: _____ (1 Samuel 1:20)

The boy who had a coat of pretty colors: _____ (Genesis 37:3)

The boy who became a king when he was seven years old: _____
(2 Chronicles 24:1)

The shepherd boy who became king: _____ (1 Samuel 16:13)

## Verse to **say**

"And [Jesus] grew and became strong . . . and the grace of God was upon him."
*Luke 2:40, NIV*

## Prayer to **pray**

Dear Jesus, when I think about you growing up as a child, just like me, I feel
_____. When I think about you being my Savior, I feel _____. Amen.

# Jesus to the Rescue

**BIBLE TRUTH**
Jesus does miracles.

**LEARNING FUN**
Foods have different tastes

**SCRIPTURE REFERENCE**
John 2:1-11

**MEMORY VERSE**
"Only God works great miracles." *Psalm 136:4, CEV*

At a wedding,
in the town of Cana,
there was a party.

People were happy.
The food tasted great.
Then something happened.

The wine was gone.
The wine jugs were empty.
What would they do?

Mary told Jesus,
"They are out of wine."
Mary wanted Jesus to help.

Jesus told the servants,
"Bring me six jars.
Fill them up with water."

A wedding guest took a cup.
He tasted the drink.
But it wasn't water!

Something happened.
The water became wine.
The wine tasted great.

Jesus did that.
He did a miracle.
This was the first time.

His friends were with him.
They saw what happened.
They believed in Jesus.

# Activities

A child quickly identifies whether or not he likes the taste of a food, but he must learn to recognize and name sweet, sour, salty, and spicy. This happens by combining a child's experience and an adult's direct teaching. For example, a child may say cinnamon is "hot" instead of spicy. Or, because he likes both a pretzel and a piece of candy, he may label both "sweet." A child is often intrigued to learn about the important role the tongue plays in taste discrimination. When talking about taste, emphasize that taste sampling should only happen when you are present.

## Game to **play**

Which foods are a different color on the inside than on the outside?
- pear
- potato
- carrot
- cucumber
- grape
- watermelon
- onion
- grapefruit
- mushroom
- apple
- pumpkin

## Questions to a**s**k

How would you describe the taste of
- a pickle?
- an orange?
- a pretzel?
- chocolate?
- a taco?

## Verse to **s**ay

"Only God works great miracles." *Psalm 136:4, CEV*

## Prayer to **pray**

Dear Jesus, I know you did wonderful things when you lived on earth. I know you do wonderful things today, such as _____. Amen.

# Many Fish

**BIBLE TRUTH**
Jesus helps his friends.

**LEARNING FUN**
Ordinals: first through fourth

**SCRIPTURE REFERENCE**
Luke 5:4-11

**MEMORY VERSE**
"The Lord is with me; he is my helper." *Psalm 118:7, NIV*

Six  men climbed into the first  boat . Six  men climbed into the second  boat . They rowed the  two boats . They threw in the first  net . They threw in the second net . They threw in the third net . They threw in the fourth net . What will happen next?

"Let's stop now," said the first man.

"I am tired," said the second man.

"Let's stop." They pulled the first  net

into the  boat . They pulled the second

 net into the  boat . They pulled the third

 net into the  boat . They pulled the

fourth  net into the  boat .

"Where are the  fish ?" asked the third

man. "There are no  fish ," said the fourth

man. Then  Jesus told the  men , "Row the

 boat here. Drop your  four nets ."

208

Many  swam into the first and the second . Many swam into the third and the fourth . There were so many , the almost began to sink.

"Stop," yelled the first man. "We have so many  , we must stop before our sinks!

The were amazed at all the that helped them catch.

# Activities

## To the parent

Young children often learn early counting skills through everyday activities. They count two dogs, three dandelions, or five cars. However, unless we help them, few children learn ordinal numbers (number defined by position or place in a sequence). Whenever you have the opportunity, help your child use the words first, second, third, and fourth. For example, you might say, "First, put on your boots. Second, put on your coat. Third, put on your scarf. Fourth, put on your mittens."

## Questions to ask

Jesus had twelve special helpers called disciples. The book of Matthew tells us that Jesus chose two fishermen to be his first disciples. What are their names? (Matthew 4:18-20)

In Matthew, these two fishermen were the second pair of disciples to follow Jesus. Who are they? (Matthew 4:21, 22)

## Song to **sing**

*Sing to the tune of "Row, Row, Row Your Boat." Encourage your child to pretend to "row" when appropriate.*

Row, row, row the boat,
Row across the sea.
Row, row, row, row,
across the Galilee.

Drop, drop, drop the net,
drop the net down deep.
Wait, wait, wait, wait –
the fish are sound asleep.

Row, row, row the boat.
"You will find some fish.
Soon, soon, soon, soon,
you'll have a tasty dish."

"No, no, no, not here"
Jesus told his friends.
"Move, move, move, move.
Now drop the net again."

Pull, pull, pull the nets
as the workday ends.
Now the men have lots of fish –
Jesus helped his friends.

Row, row, row the boat,
rowing oh so slow,
loaded down with flopping fish;
now back home they go.

## Verse to **say**

"The Lord is with me; he is my helper." *Psalm 118:7, NIV*

## Prayer to **pray**

Dear Jesus, when I hear wonderful stories about all the fish in the sea, then I'm especially happy that you help and care about me. Amen.

# Matthew, Mr. Money

**BIBLE TRUTH**
We should follow Jesus.

**LEARNING FUN**
Rote counting 0–10

**SCRIPTURE REFERENCE**
Mark 2:14

**MEMORY VERSE**
"I obey your word instead of following a way that leads to trouble."
*Psalm 119:101, CEV*

"**Z**ero, **one,** this will be fun.
**Two, three,** let me see.
**Four, five, six,** I must count quick.
**Seven, eight, nine,** I'm doing fine.
End at **ten,** and count again."

Over and over Matthew repeated his counting song. Matthew was a tax collector, and he loved counting money. Matthew counted some money for the government and some money for himself. Matthew loved money more than anything else. He liked the clink, clink sound of the coins dropping in his bag. He liked the smooth, round shape of the coins in his hand. He even liked the smell of his money bags.

"**Zero, one,** this will be fun.
**Two, three,** let me see.
**Four, five, six,** I must count quick.
**Seven, eight, nine,** I'm doing fine.
End at **ten,** and count again."

Over and over Matthew repeated the rhyme. When he was counting his money at home, Matthew sang with a booming voice. But on days like today, when people crowded around, Matthew sang the words to himself.

Matthew was happy whenever he had money. Today, Matthew was very happy. Many people were lined up at his table near the lake. Today he would hear the clink of many coins.

Matthew looked up to take money from the next person in line, but the man didn't put coins on the table. He didn't even plop down a money pouch. The man just stood there, looking straight at Matthew. The man was Jesus.

Quietly, Jesus said, "Come with me."

Matthew felt the money bags leaning heavily against his legs. Matthew saw the coins glisten on the table in front of him. He saw the line of people stretched before him, waiting to give him money. He thought of all the money he had stored up at home, but Matthew knew what he must do.

Tripping over the bags of coins as he stood, Matthew came around to the front of the table. Leaving the money bags and even the coins on the table, Matthew followed Jesus.

Later that day, Matthew had a new counting song, which he sang wherever he went.

"My money bags are empty,
and that's just fine with me.
I'm busy helping Jesus
count people, don't you see?"

# Activities

In previous generations, teaching about money was relatively easy: a parent might dump out a pocketful of change and encourage a child to identify, match, and count the coins. But in today's world of virtual cash and ATM's, parents must make a conscious effort to help a child touch and talk about coins and cash. Encourage your child to identify coins by feeling size and shape in a purse or pocket. Talk about the pictures on bills. Permit your child to accept change at a register and verify the correct amount. Let your child fill his offering envelope. Also look for other opportunities to give your child concrete experiences with money.

## Game to play

Matthew stopped counting money and followed the leader—Jesus! Play follow the leader with your child. Let him begin by being the follower and then the leader. When your child leads, encourage him to do various movements with his arms, legs, hands, feet, and head.

## Questions to **ask**

Which would you rather have
- seven pennies or a nickel?
- one quarter or four nickels?
- one dime or thirteen pennies?
- three dimes or one quarter?
- one dime or two nickels?

## Verse to **say**

"I obey your word instead of following a way that leads to trouble."
*Psalm 119:101, CEV*

## Prayer to **pray**

Dear Jesus, help me to follow you in what I do. Amen.

# Empty Hands, Full Hearts

**BIBLE TRUTH**
We can tell about
Jesus.

**LEARNING FUN**
Zero (the empty set)

**SCRIPTURE REFERENCE**
Mark 6:6-10

**MEMORY VERSE**
"Go to the people of all
nations and make them my
disciples." *Matthew 28:19, CEV*

The Lord, he sent us out to teach.
He sent us out in twos.
We could not take a single thing
except our clothes and shoes.

We took along a walking stick,
but not an extra coat.
We did not pack a loaf of bread
or ride upon a goat.

The Lord, he sent us out to teach –
we each were in a pair.
We went out just the two of us.
We walked from here to there.

We did not have a single coin
of extra cash along,
yet walking down the road we sang
our thankful little song.

We carry nothing, zero, zip.
We come with empty hand,
but we bring news of Jesus Christ
across the whole, big land.

Our hands are empty, nothing there,
but hearts are full of joy.
We share the message Jesus gives
to every girl and boy.

# Activities

## To the parent

"None," "nothing," and "empty" are some of the first synonyms a child learns for the empty set. Counting often begins with the first numeral, so a child might not even hear the word "zero" until he is taught formal arithmetic concepts. To expand your child's math vocabulary, substitute the word "zero" for "nothing" during casual conversation. For example, you might say, "We have zero eggs. That means there isn't a single egg in the carton."

## Game to play

Jesus sent his disciples out in pairs. How many pairs can you find?

What do you think the disciples said in each of the places?

## Questions to **ask**

Would you rather have
- a loose tooth or an empty space?
- five presents or zero presents?
- five ants at the picnic or no ants?
- three thank-you notes to write or no thank-you notes to write?
- five things in a backpack or nothing in a backpack?

## Verse to **say**

"Go to the people of all nations and make them my disciples."
*Matthew 28:19, CEV*

## Prayer to **pray**

Dear Jesus, for giving me the words to say to tell about you every day, I thank you now for helping me to share your love for all to see. Amen.

# Two Plus Five

**BIBLE TRUTH**
God gives us what we need.

**LEARNING FUN**
Addition

**SCRIPTURE REFERENCE**
John 6:1-15

**MEMORY VERSE**
"Everyone depends on you . . . you provide them with food." *Psalm 145:15, CEV*

Does anyone here have food?" Andrew asked. He and Jesus' other helpers moved among the people, hoping someone would have food to share.

"Does anyone here have food?" Andrew asked again. Jesus had been teaching all day and everyone was getting hungry.

"Does anyone here have food?" the men asked, wandering through the crowd.

"I have a basket of food," a young voice popped up. Andrew moved toward the boy who had spoken.

"See," said the boy. He opened his basket to show Andrew. "I have five small barley loaves and two little fish. Seven things to eat," the boy proudly counted.

Andrew and the boy walked toward Jesus and his other helpers.

"Here is a young boy with five small barley loaves plus two little fish," said Andrew.

"That's seven things to eat," the boy added. "I will share with you."

"Thank you," said Andrew. "But seven bites of food will feed a little boy like you, not a whole crowd. There are thousands of people here."

Yet Jesus took the five small loaves of barley bread. He blessed the bread. His helpers shared the bread with everyone.

Jesus took the two small fish. He blessed the fish. His helpers shared the fish with everyone.

All five thousand people had plenty to eat. Jesus' helpers walked through the crowd and gathered the leftovers. There were twelve baskets of barley bread left over.

Everyone was amazed that Jesus had fed thousands of people with just seven things to eat: five small loaves and two little fish.

# Activities

## To the **parent**

A child distinguishes between "few" and "many," "more" and "less," and has a clear understanding of numbers and their meaning before he begins to add numerals. A child needs many experiences with counting in sequence and counting to a specified number before he can add two distinct groups of numbers to come up with a sum. Mathematical concepts develop slowly and over a lengthy period of time. Help your child get much-needed practice with numerical concepts by counting plates for supper, people at a party, and toys on a shelf.

## Game to **play**

*Encourage your child to fill in the blanks.*

Two plus five, that makes seven;
Jesus held the food toward _____ (heaven).

One fish plus one fish makes two;
Two is a couple and less than a _____ (few).

"Five little loaves of barley bread,
that's what I have," the young boy _____ (said).

One, two, three, four, five, six, seven,
that is four less than _____ (eleven).

# Song to **sing**

*Sing to the tune of "Kum Bah Yah."*

There are people, Lord, sitting here.
There are people, Lord, sitting here.
There are people, Lord, sitting here,
Many people sitting here.

They are hungry, Lord, sitting here.
They are hungry, Lord, sitting here.
They are hungry, Lord, sitting here,
Many people sitting here.

Take five loaves of bread and two fish.
Take five loaves of bread and two fish.
Take five loaves of bread and two fish,
Many people sitting here.

Bless the food, my Lord, bless the food.
Bless the food, my Lord, bless the food.
Bless the food, my Lord, bless the food,
Many people sitting here.

All have eaten, Lord. We praise you.
All have eaten, Lord. We praise you.
All have eaten, Lord. We praise you,
Many people thank you, Lord.

# Verse to **say**

"Everyone depends on you . . . you provide them with food."
*Psalm 145:15, CEV*

# Prayer to **pray**

Dear Jesus, I like a lot of foods. I especially like to eat _____. Thank you for giving me good food that I need. Amen.

# Pay Up, Peter!

Peter felt in his pocket. It was totally empty. He could only feel the **roughness** of the cloth. There wasn't a single coin in his pocket. Then he felt around in his leather bag. Perhaps he would feel a coin or two there. But he only felt the **smooth** leather bag.

"Well," Peter thought to himself, "perhaps the tax collectors won't see us."

But they did. The tax collectors came to Peter and asked, "Does Jesus pay taxes?"

Peter nodded yes. He felt again in his pocket. It was definitely empty. He felt again in his money bag—no **smooth**, round coins there. Where would he and Jesus get the money to pay the tax collectors?

Jesus and Peter talked about the tax. Jesus said, "We don't want to cause trouble, so we need to pay the money."

Peter turned his pocket inside out to show Jesus it was completely empty. He even turned over his money bag. Not a single coin dropped out.

"Look, Jesus," he said, "how can I pay the tax?"

Jesus told him, "Toss your fishing line over there into the water. Pull out the first fish you hook. When you open its mouth, you'll find a coin to pay your taxes and mine."

Peter did just what Jesus said. He threw his line into the lake. Almost immediately, he had a nibble. When the fish was hooked, he grabbed onto the **rough** scales. He opened the fish's mouth to take out the hook. He also took out a coin.

Peter turned the **smooth** coin over and over in his hands. Then he went to pay the tax in order to obey the leaders.

# Activities

Tactile discrimination, as highlighted in this story by contrasting rough and smooth, is typically one of the least developed areas of early childhood learning. Initially, a child makes three common mistakes which self-correct through practice and experience. He may think that "rough" and "smooth" describe the objects, and are not simply qualities of an object; he may confuse hard and soft with rough and smooth; and he may make up his own adjectives, such as "bumpety" or "nubby."

## Game to **play**

Name something that feels
- rough
- pointed
- smooth
- brittle
- crumbly

T is for textures, bumpy or smooth.
H is for my hands, which I use for touching.
A is for furry animals that I pet.
N is for night, when I can't see but I still can feel.
K is for kisses; they feel best of all.
S is for saying "Thanks, Jesus," for a world of squeezy, spiky, slimy, stretchy, sharp, springy, slippery, shaggy things to feel.

## Verse to **say**

"Obey the rulers who have authority over you." *Romans 13:1, CEV*

## Prayer to **pray**

Dear Jesus, please watch over the leaders of our country. Help them make good laws. Amen.

# Come to Jesus

**BIBLE TRUTH**
Jesus loves children.

**LEARNING FUN**
Language patterns

**SCRIPTURE REFERENCE**
Mark 10:13-16

**MEMORY VERSE**
"God is love."
*1 John 4:16, NIV*

This story uses the echo format and rhythm of the familiar children's chant, "We're Going on a Bear Hunt." Sit cross-legged on the floor. During the three verses, encourage your child to tap the rhythm against the floor, then sit quietly during the interludes. The italics indicate what your child should repeat.

We're going to see Jesus.
*We're going to see Jesus.*
Jesus is our teacher.
*Jesus is our teacher.*
Jesus is our best friend.
*Jesus is our best friend.*
We're going to see Jesus.
*We're going to see Jesus.*

*Interlude*
Stop!
Jesus is too busy.
He has no time for you.

236

237

*Verse Two*
"No, let the children see me.
*No, let the children see me.*
I want to bless the children.
*I want to bless the children.*
The children are important.
*The children are important.*
I will bless the children.
*I will bless the children.*"

*Interlude*
Come,
Jesus will see you.
Jesus will bless you.

*Verse Three*
I know Jesus loves me.
*I know Jesus loves me.*
He thinks I'm important.
*He thinks I'm important.*
Jesus is my Savior.
*Jesus is my Savior.*
I know Jesus loves me.
*I know Jesus loves me.*

# Activities

Talking and listening seem like such simple processes, but just like other aspects of language, they are actually very complex. In this story, when your child hears and then echoes the line, "We're going to see Jesus," he will copy your rhythmic pattern. After reading this story the first time, ask your child to close his eyes during the second reading. Even if your child peeks, closing his eyes will help him focus his listening on the sounds and rhythms of your words.

## To **talk** about

*Young children view Jesus as a best friend before they understand the concept of Savior. Use these questions to further explore the meaning of friendship.*

A friend is someone who _____.

When I want to be friends with someone, I _____.

I share with a friend when _____.

When a friend smiles at me, I feel _____.

I can be friendly by _____.

## Game to play

*Rhyming and repetition of a basic sentence structure are two literary devices often used to help a child hear and practice language patterns. After you read a line or two of the section below, your child will naturally chime in when you reach the repetitive words in the sentences.*

The sky is oh so pretty: blue, blue, blue.
Now come along with me: do, do, do.

We're going to see Jesus: walk, walk, walk.
We're going to hear Jesus: talk, talk, talk.

When will we see Jesus? By noon, noon, noon.
Will that be very long? Soon, soon, soon.

Let's hurry now and run: race, race, race.
Finally we've come to the place, place, place.

Look beyond the people: see, see, see.
At whom is Jesus smiling? Me, me, me.

## Verse to say

"God is love." *1 John 4:16, NIV*

## Prayer to pray

Dear Jesus, thank you for loving me. Amen.

# Who Is My Neighbor?

### BIBLE TRUTH
We should help each other.

### LEARNING FUN
Focused listening

### SCRIPTURE REFERENCE
Luke 10:29-37

### MEMORY VERSE
"You show love for others by truly helping them, and not merely by talking about it."
1 John 3:18, CEV

**As you read the story, ask the highlighted questions as indicated and pause to allow your child to answer them.**

One day when Jesus was teaching, someone asked him, "What is the most important thing for me to do?"

Jesus answered, "Love God with all your heart and soul and strength and mind, and love your neighbor just as much as you love yourself."

"Who is my neighbor?" the man asked Jesus. (The man asked this because he didn't really want to love everybody.) Jesus told this story to answer the man's question:

Walk, walk, walk. A man walked down the road. Suddenly robbers jumped out at him. They hit him. They took all his money. The man was left lying in the road.

Were the robbers good neighbors?

Walk, walk, walk. A priest walked down the road. He saw the man lying there. He walked past on the other side.

Was the priest a good neighbor?

Walk, walk, walk. A priest's helper walked down the road. He saw the man lying there. He walked right past.

Was the priest's helper a good neighbor?

Walk, walk, walk. A man from another country walked down the road. He saw the man lying there. He stopped to bandage his wounds. He lifted the hurt man onto his donkey and took him to get help.

Was the man from another country a good neighbor?

The man who asked Jesus, "Who is my neighbor?" knew that the man in the story who helped was a good neighbor. "If someone from another country is my neighbor, then everyone is my neighbor," he thought.

Jesus said to the man, "Now you know how to be a good neighbor, too."

# Activities

Children who listen frequently to stories develop better language and higher reading comprehension skills than those who don't hear stories. Part of the reason is a child who listens to a story must focus intently—the child must pay attention to find out what happens. This directly contrasts what happens in real-life experiences. For example, when a child helps someone set the dinner table, he is face-to-face with action that is happening right now. He can mentally tune in and tune out and still keep up with the situation. However, hearing this story of the good Samaritan removes the action beyond his reality: he must listen to know what goes on. This focused attention is one of the strengths children develop when they hear someone read aloud.

## Questions to **ask**

A neighbor is someone who helps. Who would be the best person to help the following people?

Who helps someone who has a sore throat?
Who helps someone who needs to mail a letter?
Who helps someone who is afraid in a storm?
Who helps someone who wants to buy a candy bar?
Who helps someone who fell off a bike?
Who helps someone who wants to learn about Jesus?
Who helps someone who is lost in the mall?

## Rhyme to say

*If you want to further encourage "focused listening" for your child, say this rhyme out loud and then ask him about some of the examples that are given on how to be a good neighbor.*

Have you seen my neighbor?
"Oh, yes," said the boy.
"There's your neighbor,
he's sharing his toy."

Have you seen my neighbor?
"Yes," my mom said.
"He's out at the feeder,
taking birdies some bread."

Have you seen my neighbor?
"Yes," said the man.
"She's watering my flowers
with her sprinkling can."

Have you seen my neighbor?
"Yes," Grandma said.
"She's kneeling to pray for all
next to her bed."

## Verse to say

"You show love for others by truly helping them, and not merely by talking about it." *1 John 3:18, CEV*

## Prayer to pray

Dear Jesus, when I pray for others and kneel down in prayer, that is one way I can tell you that I care. Amen.

# The Noisy Cook

**BIBLE TRUTH**
We should learn about Jesus.

**LEARNING FUN**
Opposites: noisy and quiet

**SCRIPTURE REFERENCE**
Luke 10:38-42

**MEMORY VERSE**
"Be quiet and know that I am God." *Psalm 46:10, ICB*

**As you read this story, encourage your child to pound the floor each time he hears the words "Noisy, noisy, noisy," and hold his fingers to his lips and say "Sh" when he hears the words "It was so quiet."**

Martha slammed the ladle to the ground. **Noisy, noisy, noisy.** "The soup isn't done," she frowned. "I didn't know it would take so long to cook."

"Our regular soup would have been fine," Mary said.

"But I wanted Jesus to have special soup," Martha said. She stirred vigorously. The soup barely simmered. **It was so quiet.**

Martha stopped stirring. Looking into the distance, she was surprised to see their guest already walking down the road. Jesus was coming!

248

"Mary, Mary," she called. "Jesus is here. But the soup's not done and the bread is still baking!"

"Calm down," laughed Mary. Welcoming their guest, Mary said, "Please come in, Jesus."

Leaving her sister and their guest, Martha stomped back outside. **Noisy, noisy, noisy.**

The flames under the soup pot had died out. **It was so quiet.** Martha cracked more sticks and tossed them into the fire. The fire roared to life. **Noisy, noisy, noisy.**

From the doorway, her sister called, "Martha, you are so noisy out there. What are you doing?"

"I'm trying to cook this slow soup, and bake our bread" Martha responded, banging the spoon yet again. **Noisy, noisy, noisy.**

"I'd call it loud soup," laughed Mary. "Martha, forget cooking. Come inside where it's nice and quiet," Mary said. "Listen to Jesus teach."

Jesus looked up. **It was so quiet.**

"The soup isn't ready and the bread will burn," Martha announced loudly. "Jesus, can't you make Mary come and help me?"

Jesus reached toward her. **It was so quiet.**

"Martha, Martha," he said softly. "You are worried about so many things. But only one thing is important," he continued. "Come, listen to me."

Martha was quiet. She was not noisy. She did not stomp. She did not bang. She did not tromp. Instead, she sat down. **It was so quiet.**

Then Mary and Martha listened to Jesus.

# Activities

## To the parent

Teaching a child about Jesus isn't always easy. Sometimes a child asks questions that are hard to answer or raises issues we haven't resolved. When that happens, an honest response is the best response. It's fine that a child knows we are still learning, too. There is nothing more wonderful than a child and an adult growing up together with Jesus.

## Questions to ask

Mary and Martha learned from Jesus. If you could ask Jesus one question, what would you ask?

Mary was wise to listen to Jesus. What does it mean to have wisdom?

Who teaches you about Jesus?

## To **talk** about

Which is louder, leaves falling or snowflakes falling?

Which is louder, a mouse squeaking or a door squeaking?

Which is louder, popcorn popping or a balloon popping?

Which is louder, pounding a drum or pounding a hammer?

## Verse to **say**

"Be quiet and know that I am God." *Psalm 46:10, ICB*

## Prayer to **pray**

Dear Jesus, help me learn more about you. Amen.

# Ten on the Road

**BIBLE TRUTH**
Thank God for his blessings.

**LEARNING FUN**
Rote Counting: 1-10

**SCRIPTURE REFERENCE**
Luke 17:11-19

**MEMORY VERSE**
"Be thankful and praise the Lord." *Psalm 100:4, CEV*

As you read this story, ask your child to count the ten men in the illustration. Have your child place his finger on each man as he counts.

As Jesus walked toward a big city, a man waved to him from across the road. Then another man appeared. Then another. Soon there was a whole group waving their hands. As Jesus walked closer, he counted ten men waving at him:

**1, 2, 3, 4, 5, 6, 7, 8, 9, 10.**

"Jesus, heal us!" the men called from across the road. The men were so sick, they could not even be with other people. Yet the men continued to wave their arms. They called to Jesus, trying to catch his attention. As he came closer, he could see all of them waving desperately:

**1, 2, 3, 4, 5, 6, 7, 8, 9, 10.**

Jesus called out to them, "Go and show yourselves to the priests." The priests could tell if the men were healed.

One by one the men realized they were healthy. Their sickness was gone. Jesus had healed them! The men started running toward the city:
1, 2, 3, 4, 5, 6, 7, 8, 9, 10.

They couldn't wait to show the priests they were healed.

But then one man turned around. He left the nine men and walked back. Bowing at Jesus' feet, he said, "You healed me. Thank you, Jesus."

# Activities

While your child may have experience counting from one to ten, you can provide opportunities for him to count from ten to one, too. Birthdays, holidays, or other special events are times we encourage a child to "count down" or count backwards. Because a young child is just beginning to understand time-related ideas, it's helpful to demonstrate mathematical concepts. Counting backwards is easy to illustrate with a paper chain. Simply cut strips of paper, one for each day of the countdown. Then your child can tape together the ends of each strip, so that the strips interlock. Each day, when he removes one strip, he will see how much closer he's coming to the special day.

## Questions to **ask**

Why do you think only one man returned to say "Thank you" to Jesus?

When did you say thank-you today?

## Song to **sing**

*Sing this rhyme to the tune of "Ten in a Bed."*

There were ten on the road,
and the first man said,
"He healed me.
He healed me."
So they all walked on,
but one went home.

There were nine on the road
and the next man said . . .

*Continue with more verses,
counting down from eight to two.*

There was one on the road,
and the last man said,
"Thank you, Jesus."

## Verse to **say**

"Be thankful and praise the Lord." *Psalm 100:4, CEV*

## Prayer to **pray**

Dear God, I am thankful for small things, like _____ and _____. I am
thankful for big things, like _____ and _____. Amen.

# Up a Tree

Tell your child: As I read this story, stand when you hear the word UP. Sit when you hear the word DOWN.

**BIBLE TRUTH**
Jesus forgives us.

**LEARNING FUN**
Directions: up and down

**SCRIPTURE REFERENCE**
Luke 19:1-10

**MEMORY VERSE**
"The Lord forgives our sins."
*Psalm 103:3, CEV*

Zacchaeus loved money. When Zacchaeus collected money, he piled the coins UP high on his table. He even stuffed the coins into bags DOWN under the table.

Sometimes Zacchaeus took extra money from people. That's why moneybags were stacked UP all over his house. Zacchaeus even dug DOWN under his floor and buried his money in clay pots!

One day, Jesus came to town. Zacchaeus wanted to see Jesus. But many other people wanted to see Jesus, too.

Zacchaeus stretched UP as tall as he could. But Zacchaeus only saw the back of the crowd. Then he scrunched DOWN to the ground. But Zacchaeus only saw hairy legs.

Then Zacchaeus had an idea. He would climb UP, then he could look DOWN. So that's what he did.

Zacchaeus climbed UP a tree. Now, he could look DOWN.

When Jesus walked under the tree, he looked UP. "Zacchaeus, come DOWN," Jesus said. "I am going to your house today."

"I climbed UP to see you," Zacchaeus explained. "But I will come DOWN to walk with you."

The men talked as they walked. The men talked as they ate. Then Jesus leaned over to hear what Zacchaeus whispered. Zacchaeus said, "I am sorry I took extra money from people."

Zacchaeus stood UP and announced to everyone, "I will give half of my money to the poor. I will give back more money than I took."

Jesus reached out toward Zacchaeus. "Sit DOWN here with me, my friend," Jesus invited. "You have done the right thing."

# Activities

## To the **parent**

A child relates easily to the story of Zacchaeus. Like a child, Zacchaeus is a physically short person who had to make choices. When compared with the life-changing decision Zacchaeus makes in this lesson, a child's choices are small; however, a child may need to do some heavy thinking to choose between a strawberry or double chocolate ice cream cone. Such "simple" choices give him valuable lessons in learning how to choose and accepting forgiveness if he makes a mistake.

## Game to **play**

*Read the following directions out loud to your child, first slowly, then quickly. Encourage him to keep up with your pace. Then switch and ask him to direct you to do "up" and "down" actions.*

Stand up.
Look down.
Look up.
Kneel down.
Get up.
Lie down.

## Song to **sing**

*Sing "Zacchaeus" together.*

Zacchaeus was a wee little man, *hands in front, right palm raised above left palm*
A wee little man was he. *bring palms closer together*
He climbed up in a sycamore tree *alternate hands in a climbing motion*
For the Lord he wanted to see. *shade eyes with right hand and look around*
And as the Savior passed that way, *"walk" fingers of right hand up left forearm*
He looked up in the tree. *shade eyes with right hand and look up*
And he said, "Zacchaeus, you come down. *speak words while shaking finger*
For I'm going to your house today. *clap hands on accented beat*
For I'm going to your house today." *clap hands on accented beat*

## Verse to **say**

"The Lord forgives our sins." *Psalm 103:3, CEV*

## Prayer to **pray**

Dear Jesus, when I make a wise choice, it feels good inside. Help me use the Bible as my lifetime guide. Amen.

# A Small Brown Donkey

**BIBLE TRUTH**
Jesus tells us what to do.

**LEARNING FUN**
Predicting what will happen next

**SCRIPTURE REFERENCE**
Luke 19:28-36

**MEMORY VERSE**
"Listen carefully to my instructions, and you will be wise." *Proverbs 8:33, CEV*

Ask your child to listen carefully while you read the story. Pause when you come to a highlighted word and encourage him to fill it in himself.

Jesus walked, walked, walked.

He said to his helpers,
"Go to the next town.
You will find a small brown donkey.
Bring it here."

"If someone asks, 'Why are you taking the small brown donkey?' Say, 'Jesus needs it.'"

Jesus' helpers walked, walked, **walked**.

They went to the next town.
They found a small brown **donkey**.

Someone asked, "Why are you taking the small **brown donkey**?"

Jesus' helpers said, "Jesus needs it."

Jesus' helpers walked, walked, **walked**.
The small, brown donkey walked, walked, **walked**.
Jesus climbed on the small **brown donkey**.
The small, brown donkey walked, walked, **walked**.
Jesus' helpers walked, **walked, walked**.
Jesus rode, rode, **rode**.

# Activities

One of the ways in which a child develops higher level listening skills is by anticipating and predicting what will come next in a familiar story or repetitive text. You can help your child practice this "active listening" skill when you read a rhyme or sing a song your child has memorized. Simply let your child complete the sentence or fill in the word. This challenges a child to stay mentally alert so he can take an active role in the listening process.

## Game to **play**

*Read these Bible verses to your child. After reading each sentence, ask your child, "What does the Bible tell us we should do?"*

"I always *pray* with joy." *Philippians 1:4, NIV*

"Children, *obey your parents.*" *Ephesians 6:1, NIV*

"*Give thanks to the Lord,* for he is good." *Psalm 136:1, NIV*

"We will *serve the Lord our God* and *obey him.*" *Joshua 24:24, NIV*

"*Do not be anxious* about anything." *Philippians 4:6, NIV*

# Song to sing

*As you sing the song "Jesus Loves Me," ask your child to supply the missing words:*

Jesus loves me! this I know,
For the Bible tells me (so);
Little ones to him belong;
They are weak, but he is (strong).
Yes, Jesus loves me!
Yes, Jesus loves (me)!
Yes, Jesus (loves me)!
The Bible tells me (so).

# Verse to say

"Listen carefully to my instructions, and you will be wise." *Proverbs 8:33, CEV*

# Prayer to pray

Dear Jesus, help me listen so I can learn more about you. Amen.

# A Rainbow Parade

**BIBLE TRUTH**
We should praise God.

**LEARNING FUN**
Colors of the rainbow

**SCRIPTURE REFERENCE**
Luke 19:36-38; John 12:13

**MEMORY VERSE**
"Praise and honor the King who rules from heaven!"
*Daniel 4:37, CEV*

Something special was going to happen!

People had gathered in Jerusalem to worship at the temple, so the city was crowded. But now, people were not gathered to pray. Instead, they started to line the streets. Something exciting was about to happen. Jesus was coming to town!

Some people laid clothes in the street. Wouldn't that have made a colorful carpet for Jesus?

An old man spread **red** fabric, as shiny as an apple on a tree. One girl put down an **orange** cloth, as fiery as a sunset. Two children laid a large **yellow** cloth, bright like the sun.

Above the street, people waved fresh **green** palm branches. Beneath the canopy of branches, a young woman spread a scarf as **blue** as the sky. And two men laid strips of royal cloth, in shades of **indigo** and **violet**, as rich as any king's robe.

Jesus would parade through a rainbow!

"Here he comes," the people shouted. Jesus' helpers cleared the way. Soon, Jesus himself came through the crowd.

"Hosanna!" people shouted. "Lord, save us!"

Jesus, sitting straight and tall, rode on a donkey. Smiling, he nodded at the crowd. Palm branches waved above him and a rainbow of colors lay at his feet.

"Jesus has come!" the crowd shouted.

"Hosanna," the people said. "Hosanna!"

# Activities

## To the **parent**

Newborns are stimulated by the high contrast of black, white, and red. That is why some crib mobiles and early toys are limited to those dramatic colors. But in only a few weeks, the infant's world explodes in a full rainbow of color. After your child has learned to name and match basic colors, help him apply skills in visual discrimination by looking for everything that is "blue like the sky" or "red like a Valentine heart."

## To **talk** about

*Remember the acronym name "ROY G. BIV" when you want to help your child identify the colors of the rainbow: red, orange, yellow, green, blue, indigo, and violet.*

Red
Orange
Yellow
Green
Blue
Indigo
Violet

## Song to **sing**

*Sing the "Doxology" together.*

Praise God, from whom all blessings flow.
Praise him, all creatures here below.
Praise him above, ye heav'nly host.
Praise Father, Son, and Holy Ghost.

## Verse to **say**

"Praise and honor the King who rules from heaven!" *Daniel 4:37, CEV*

## Prayer to **pray**

Dear Jesus, thank you for reminding me to celebrate your colorful world. I especially like the color _____ because _____. Amen.

# A Good Lesson

**BIBLE TRUTH**
God wants us to help each other.

**LEARNING FUN**
Visual tracking

**SCRIPTURE REFERENCE**
John 13:1-17

**MEMORY VERSE**
"I have set the example, and you should do for each other exactly what I have done for you." *John 13:15, CEV*

One by one, the men climbed the stairs. One by one, they greeted each other.

Tonight was a special night. Jesus and his helpers were gathering in a room alone, away from the crowded and noisy streets. They were going to have dinner together.

Talking quietly among themselves, the men thought of all they had learned from Jesus. They had traveled together for a long time. Jesus was their friend, but more than that, he was their teacher. The men were always learning something new.

As the men gathered around the table, Jesus took off his coat. Then he wrapped a towel around his waist like an apron. "Why is Jesus doing that?" the men wondered.

Jesus poured water into a large bowl. Then he went to every helper and washed his feet.

One of his helpers said, "Jesus, my feet are filthy. You don't have to wash my feet."

But Jesus kept washing feet.

After all his helpers had clean feet, Jesus took off his apron and put his coat back on. Then he told them why he had washed everyone's feet.

"I am your teacher and Lord," Jesus began. His helpers nodded. He was right.

"Tonight, I wanted to show you how to care for each other," Jesus said. "I showed you how to be kind. Now you can be kind to each other in the same way."

The men sitting around the table thought about that lesson. Once again, Jesus had been a good teacher.

# Activities

## To the **parent**

Before becoming a fluent reader, a child's eyes must be trained to move from the upper left-hand corner of a page, down the page, to the lower right-hand corner. Your child can practice this element of "visual tracking" in the story activity. Also, look for everyday opportunities to train your child in this pre-reading skill. For example, before your child copies a grocery list to practice writing or prints a letter to Grandma, put a star or dot in the upper left-hand corner of the page to indicate his starting point. Soon he will automatically glance toward that corner whenever he begins to read or write on a page.

## Verse to **say**

"I have set the example, and you should do for each other exactly what I have done for you." *John 13:15, CEV*

## Prayer to **pray**

Dear Jesus, thank you for showing me how to care for others. Thank you most of all for showing me the way to heaven. Amen.

Ask your child to retell the story by tracing his finger along the "road" and explaining what happens at each illustration. As he does this, he will move from top to bottom, and left to right. This will help reinforce the skill of visual tracking.

# Sounds of Silence

## BIBLE TRUTH
Jesus died for us.

## LEARNING FUN
Qualities of sound: loud and soft

## SCRIPTURE REFERENCE
John 19:16-30; Luke 23:34

## MEMORY VERSE
"This man really was the Son of God!" *Mark 15:39, CEV*

**Read the highlighted type in a louder or softer than normal voice as indicated by the word.**

Mary sobbed. Her son, Jesus, was going to die. During the last days, huge crowds had **shouted** to leaders and officials. **Yelling** people had jammed into the streets. **Noisy** mobs had gathered. **Shouts** against Jesus filled the air.

But now, there was **silence**. There wasn't a single sound. Everything was **quiet** on the hill where Jesus was dying.

Everything was **quiet** until Jesus started to speak. He prayed to God. "Father, forgive these people, for they don't know what they are doing." Even while he was dying, Jesus prayed for his enemies.

Again, there was **silence**. There wasn't a single sound.

Everything was **quiet** until Jesus started to speak. He told his helper John, "Take care of my mother, Mary." Even while he was dying Jesus cared for others.

Again there was **silence**. There wasn't a single sound.

Everything was **quiet** until Jesus started to speak. He told everyone, "It is finished."

And there wasn't another sound.

# Activities

We love to see a smiling child, so we celebrate when shouts of joy fill the air. Because we eagerly encourage a child to express his happy emotions, we are quick to excuse a little extra noise. Although we might be tempted to immediately stop shouts of frustration or quiet a child's angry yell, we should encourage him to share when he feels sad or unhappy. A child may work out such feelings by kicking a soccer ball, pumping a swing, or riding a bike. We should also take every opportunity to help a child *talk* about emotions. Sometimes, a child will vent more easily if we talk first. For example, you might say, "I am sad when I hear about Jesus' death. Sometimes I'd like to skip that story. But if I did that, I couldn't feel doubly happy when we get to the resurrection story. That's when I really want to shout for joy!"

## Rhyme to **say**

Who made the birds to sing so sweet?
Who made the food I crunch to eat?
Who made the dogs that bark and howl?
Who made the hooting, sleepy owl?
God did.
God created a world full of sound.
Listen, now what do you hear?

Who made the thunder, booming loud?
Who made the talking, chatting crowd?
Who gave me ears that I can hear
the sounds so noisy and so dear?
God did.
God created a world full of sound.
Listen, now what do you hear?

*Today, ask your child to pray while holding two fingers together in the shape of a cross. Then shine a flashlight against a wall, so the shadow of his fingers is visible on the wall. The cross will be enlarged in the beam of the light. Seeing an empty cross in this way can remind a child that Jesus did not stay dead. He rose from the dead!*

*Your child can experiment with standing close to the wall and then moving farther and farther back. Share with your child that Jesus died because he loves us. As your child steps back, he can talk about all the additional people Jesus loves.*

When I stand close to the wall, the cross looks small. Jesus loves me.

When I take one step back from the wall, the cross looks a little bigger. Jesus loves me and my family.

When I take two steps back from the wall, the cross looks even bigger. Jesus love me, my family, and _____.

When I take three steps back from the wall, the cross looks even bigger. Jesus loves me, my family, _____, and _____.

"This man really was the Son of God!" *Mark 15:39, CEV*

Dear Jesus, when I hear about your death, I feel _____. Thank you, Jesus, for doing this for me.

# Come See, Go Tell

**BIBLE TRUTH**
Jesus is alive.

**LEARNING FUN**
Qualities of speed

**SCRIPTURE REFERENCE**
Matthew 28:1-11

**MEMORY VERSE**
"I will be with you always."
*Matthew 28:20, CEV*

To dramatize the contrast between standing still and moving fast, ask your child to run in place as you read the italicized verses.

*Go, Mary, go.*
*The sky will soon be light.*
*Faster, Mary, faster.*
*The day will soon dawn bright.*

The woman stopped.
The ground shook.
The cave was empty.

*Go, Mary, go.*
*What an awful day.*
*Quickly, Mary, quickly.*
*The Lord has gone away.*

"Stop," said an angel.
"Do not be afraid.
The Lord has risen."

*Go, Mary, go.*
*He is alive and well.*
*Run, Mary, run.*
*You've seen and now go tell.*

# Activities

The message of the first Easter can be summed up for a child in four words: "Come see. Go tell." When telling the resurrection story to children, the emphasis should be placed on the fact that Jesus is alive and with us. Often, a child who focuses on the core meaning of Easter can share this good news more effectively than an adult who may get sidetracked by focusing on "deeper" issues, interpretations, or applications. With whom can your child share the news that Jesus is alive?

## Song to sing

*Sing to the tune of "The Farmer in the Dell."*

Jesus is alive.
Jesus is alive.
I'm so very happy –
Jesus is alive.

I will go and tell.
I will go and tell.
I will go tell everyone that
Jesus is alive.

## Questions to a**s**k

Which moves faster:
- A fish or a pig?
- A car or a bike?
- A turtle or a cat?
- A falling leaf or falling snowflake?
- A worm or an ant?
- A cloud or a plane?

## Verse to **s**ay

"I will be with you always." *Matthew 28:20, CEV*

## Prayer to **pray**

Dear Jesus, I'm glad you rose on Easter. That means you are always with me. Amen.

# High, Higher, Highest

**BIBLE TRUTH**
Jesus went to heaven and is coming again.

**LEARNING FUN**
Height comparisons

**SCRIPTURE REFERENCE**
Acts 1:6-11

**MEMORY VERSE**
"Jesus has been taken to heaven. But he will come back." *Acts 1:11, CEV*

Ask your child to say "High on the mountain" (the highlighted words of each verse) when you point or nod your head.

High on the mountain,
outside the city,
Jesus met his helpers.

High on the mountain,
Jesus reminded them,
"Tell people about me."

High on the mountain,
Jesus rose higher.
Jesus rose up into heaven.

High on the mountain,
Jesus' helpers looked
even higher into the sky.

High on the mountain,
angels came down
from heaven to earth.

High on the mountain,
the angels said,
"Jesus is in heaven,
but he will come back."

# Activities

Sharing a story can be a highly interactive activity, even if a child does not know how to read. Your child might participate by repeating a refrain, identifying letters or sight words on a page, or predicting what will happen next. These and other activities guarantee a high level of mental, visual, and auditory involvement, elements that contribute to effective language learning.

## Questions to ask

Which is higher, the top of a car or the top of a building?

Which is higher, the grass or the clouds?

Which is higher, my waist or my chin?

Which is higher, the basement or the roof?

Which is higher, a mountain or a seashore?

Which is higher, the top of a flower or the top of a tree?

## To **talk** about

*In this Bible story, angels told Jesus' helpers that Jesus had gone to heaven. What else can you learn about angels?*

How do angels help? (Psalm 91:11, 12 – they protect)

What do angels do in heaven? (Hebrews 1:6 – they praise and serve God)

How many angels are there? (Revelation 5:11; Daniel 7:10 – more than we can count!)

How strong is an angel? (Matthew 28:2; 2 Kings 19:35 – strong enough to move a huge stone and destroy an army)

## Verse to **say**

"Jesus has been taken to heaven. But he will come back." *Acts 1:11, CEV*

## Prayer to **pray**

Dear Jesus, I know that you are in heaven, and someday I will see you. Thank you for sending your angels to be with me until then. Amen.

# From Nothing to Something

**BIBLE TRUTH**
Praise God for the wonderful things he does.

**LEARNING FUN**
Opposites: something and nothing

**SCRIPTURE REFERENCE**
Acts 3:1-10

**MEMORY VERSE**
"Praise God, the Father of our Lord Jesus Christ. God is so good." *1 Peter 1:3, CEV*

As you read this story, encourage your child to hold his palms up when you say the word "something." Ask him to turn his hands downward when you say the word "nothing."

Some men gently carried their friend to the Beautiful Gate. Each day, they brought the crippled man to this door outside the temple. The crippled man was very poor. Because he had no money, he sat on the ground and begged.

"I have **nothing**, sir. Please give me **something**," he begged a man who passed through the Beautiful Gate.

"I have **nothing**, madam. Please give me **something**," he begged.

Yet often, people who had a great deal of money would simply walk by the man who had nothing.

One day, Jesus' helpers Peter and John came to the Beautiful Gate. Once again, the crippled man said, "I have **nothing**. Could you give me **something**?"

Peter and John stopped and looked at him.

Peter said, "I don't have any silver or gold money to give you. But I will give you something very valuable. In the name of Jesus Christ, get up and walk."

At once, the poor crippled man stood up. He started walking. As he walked with Peter and John into the temple, the man could not stop jumping and praising God.

"I had **nothing**," shouted the man. "Now I have **something** wonderful: I can walk. Praise God! Praise God!"

Everyone recognized the crippled beggar and saw that he was now jumping around.

People were surprised that a man who had **nothing** had received **something** so amazing.

And the beggar continued to praise God.

# Activities

A child's level of understanding of this story represents a point on his developmental spiritual journey, for this lesson reflects a fact we accept on faith. Faith has been defined as believing without seeing. God can bless us when, by faith, we open our lives and hearts to him. Some Christians hold uplifted hands to God as a way to show gratitude for the many blessings they receive through open hands and hearts, as your child is encouraged to do during the reading of this story.

## Rhyme to ſay

*Encourage your child to do the actions suggested by this rhyme. Say the rhyme several times, getting progressively faster each time.*

I praise God with my hands,
clap, clap, clap.
I praise God with my feet,
tap, tap, tap.
I praise God with my voice,
and shout hooray.
My hands, my feet, my voice
praise God every day.

## Game to **play**

*Ask your child to point thumbs-down when the sentence refers to something empty, or "nothing," and point thumbs-up when the sentence refers to something full. Discuss the sentences that might have two correct answers. For example, the kitty's dish may be empty (because she ate all her food), but her tummy may be full!*

Kitty ate all her food.
The shopping cart was overloaded.
The bubble bath drained out of the tub.
I hear coins jingling in your pocket.
Only a broken shell was left in the bird's nest.
You colored on every page of the coloring book.

## Verse to **say**

"Praise God, the Father of our Lord Jesus Christ. God is so good."
*1 Peter 1:3, CEV*

## Prayer to **pray**

Dear Jesus, when I'm sick and feeling bad, when I'm angry, feeling mad, when I'm hungry, tired, too, I can always pray to you. Amen.

# Songs From Prison

**BIBLE TRUTH**
God takes care of us.

**LEARNING FUN**
Qualities of sound and movement

**SCRIPTURE REFERENCE**
Acts 16:22-34

**MEMORY VERSE**
"You gave me a new song, a song of praise to you."
Psalm 40:3, CEV

C*lank, clank, clank.* The ankle chains banged heavily as Paul and Silas stumbled down the jail stairs.

*Clank, clank, clank.* The jailer led the men down to the basement. Then the jailer left. His footsteps echoed loudly in the dungeon, then faded away.

Paul and Silas couldn't see each other in the darkness, but they spoke softly together. Then, just before midnight, the two men began to sing. They sang softly at first, but more boldly when other prisoners started to listen.

"How can you sing praise to God from prison?" a voice yelled through the darkness.

"God loves us," Silas called back.

"He's with us here," Paul called. "He's with you, too."

And God's helpers sang even louder.

Suddenly, their voices were drowned out by a rumbling deep under the earth. The walls split behind Paul and Silas. The chains clanked off the prisoners. The prison doors banged open. The earthquake shook the prison off the foundation. Noise and confusion were everywhere.

The jailer panicked when he saw the prison had collapsed and his prisoners might have escaped, but Paul and Silas called out, "Don't worry. We're here."

The jailer lit a torch and stumbled down the collapsed stairway. Kneeling before the two men of God, he asked softly, "How can I be saved by Jesus?"

Paul and Silas said, "Have faith in Jesus as your Lord, and you will be saved."

Then the jailer led the two prisoners through the darkness to his own home. Paul and Silas changed into clean clothes. They ate good food. And the only sound heard in the jailer's home was Paul teaching about Jesus.

# Activities

A child naturally responds to music with movement. Encourage your child to dance to the opening song of a children's video, hum with a nighttime tape, or sing along with the radio. Some research suggests spontaneous movement to music peaks just before a child enters a formal classroom setting. Apparently, peer pressures to conform and a success-driven culture combine to discourage such creative expression. Enjoyment should be the primary goal of music and movement during the early years. However, because children respond so naturally to rhythm, music can be used to build vocabulary, reinforce concepts, and foster memorization.

## Questions to **ask**

What is the difference between noise and music?

Do you make a louder noise by tapping your feet or clapping your hands?

Which do you like better, fast songs or slow songs?

## Rhyme to say

*Encourage your child to do the actions suggested by the following rhyme.*

Feet stomp,
feet run,
feet stamp
to have some fun.

Arms stretch,
arms swing,
arms reach up
to praise our King.

Hands shake,
hands clap,
hands are quiet
in my lap.

## Verse to say

"You gave me a new song, a song of praise to you." *Psalm 40:3, CEV*

## Prayer to pray

Dear Jesus, my favorite song to sing about you is _____. When I sing about you, I feel _____. Amen.

# The Long Sermon

**BIBLE TRUTH**
We should listen to stories about Jesus.

**LEARNING FUN**
Time of day

**SCRIPTURE REFERENCE**
Acts 20:7-12

**MEMORY VERSE**
"Anyone who belongs to God will listen to his message." *John 8:47, CEV*

I'm leaving in the morning, so I might speak for a long time tonight," Paul told his listeners. Many in the crowd smiled. They were happy that Paul would teach a long lesson. People were so eager to hear Paul speak about Jesus that they had filled every available space.

One young man, Eutychus, even squeezed into a third floor window ledge. But Eutychus was happy. From his perch he could hear Paul and also watch a beautiful sunset. As Paul began to speak, Eutychus watched the sun turn to orange, and then to a fiery red. Finally, the sun slipped completely away. Darkness came quickly. Then Eutychus turned his full attention to Paul.

Seven o'clock.

Eight o'clock.

Nine o'clock. Paul preached on and on.

Ten o'clock.

Eleven o'clock.

Midnight came. And Paul still preached. Sitting on his perch high above the ground, Eutychus grew drowsy. His head nodded. Eutychus tried to keep his eyes open so he could stay awake and learn from Paul. But finally he fell completely asleep.

"Someone fell!" a person shouted. "That young man fell out the window."

Eutychus lay silently on the ground, three floors below the window. People rushed to help, but Eutychus was not breathing.

The crowd stepped aside as Paul bent over the body. He took the young man in his arms and announced, "Don't worry. He's alive."

Paul then continued to teach. He finished speaking just as dawn was breaking the next morning. Paul had preached a sermon all through the night. And Eutychus's friends took him home. They were so glad that he was alive. And everyone was glad they had heard Paul talk about Jesus.

# Activities

Although adults are extremely time sensitive, a child is often uninterested in time-related concepts. Although a child wants to know what will happen next, routine, not time of day, is the frame of reference. Using appropriate terminology such as morning, noon, and evening will help a child mentally outline the day. Understanding about longer units of time—tomorrow, next month, or the historical past—will occur gradually and most easily when tied to concrete places, people, or events (for example, when Jesus lived or when Grandma was a little girl).

## Questions to **ask**

What time do you get up in the morning?
What time do you eat lunch?
What time do you read a book?
What time do you take a bath?
What time do you go to bed?
How could you tell what time it was if you didn't have a clock?
What is the latest you've ever stayed up at night?
What is the difference between morning and night?
What is nice about going to sleep?

## To **talk** about

*If your child goes to church, and if you talk about the Bible in your home, your child has many opportunities to hear stories about Jesus, and in many different ways. You and your child can complete these sentences together, sharing your answers.*

I hear people sing about Jesus when . . .
I listen to someone read about Jesus when . . .
I watch someone act like Jesus when . . .
I learn about Jesus when . . .
I do what Jesus says when . . .

## Verse to **say**

"Anyone who belongs to God will listen to his message." *John 8:47, CEV*

## Prayer to **pray**

Dear Jesus, I can learn about you in the morning when I wake up. I can learn about you at lunchtime when the day is halfway over. I can learn about you at night when I go to sleep. Thank you for helping me learn about you the whole day through. Amen.

# Ride Through the Night

While you read the story, count the men by tens. When you are done, help your child do the same.

**BIBLE TRUTH**
God protects us.

**LEARNING FUN**
Counting by multiples

**SCRIPTURE REFERENCE**
Acts 23:12-31

**MEMORY VERSE**
"With your powerful arm you protect me from every side." *Psalm 139:5, CEV*

**Ten, twenty, thirty, forty.** More than forty men squeezed into the small room. They were upset that Paul had been teaching about Jesus.

"Let's get that guy, Paul," said one man. "He shouldn't be teaching about Jesus."

"Yes," said another. "Let's agree not to eat or drink anything until we get him."

**Ten, twenty, thirty, forty.** The men nodded their heads.

**Ten, twenty, thirty, forty** plus one: someone else listened to their plans. Paul's nephew heard what the men said.

Paul's nephew told an army officer, "Forty men are going to capture my uncle. Please help him."

The army officer took Paul's nephew to the commander. Paul's nephew said, "Forty men are going to capture my uncle. Please help him."

The commander listened and whispered, "Let's keep this a secret." Then the commander thought about this news.

"**Ten, twenty, thirty, forty**," he said to himself. "That's a lot of men. I will need to protect Paul with more men than that." And he did.

By nine o'clock that same night, two hundred soldiers gathered around Paul. Seventy soldiers rode on horseback. Paul climbed on a horse, too. And in the cover of darkness, surrounded by the soldiers, Paul rode to safety.

**Ten, twenty, thirty, forty** men — not one of them captured Paul!

# Activities

## To the **parent**

Counting by multiples, most commonly by twos or tens, is an arithmetic skill a child formally learns only after he has a full understanding of one-to-one correspondence (matching a number of objects with a specific numeral). However, a child is often informally exposed to fast-track counting long before that time. Typically, a child responds with amazement when he observes a quick count, for example, when he hears a parent counting party bags by twos or school picnic favors by tens. When your child wants to "count like that, too," encourage that enthusiasm as he picks up the rhythm. However, know that until he comprehends one-to-one correspondence, counting by multiples is merely a fun activity, not a reflection of skill competence.

## Game to **play**

Give your child practice using one-to-one correspondence before he counts multiples. For example, ask your child to count picnic forks individually from one to five. Then have your child set the forks aside in groups of five. Finally, quick-count the total number of forks by multiples of five. You will find other opportunities to give your child math practice when tallying books on a shelf, pencils in a can, or socks in a drawer. This experience of using math helps your child connect the learning of school skills with everyday life.

## Song to Sing

*Sing to the tune of "Old MacDonald Had a Farm." Be sure to do the activities the song suggests!*

God protects me every day,
everywhere I go.
God protects me here and there;
that I surely know.
So I thank you, Lord, and I shout,
    "Praise God."
Let me clap, let me stomp, let me
    spin around now.
God protects me, that I know,
everywhere I go.

God protects me every day,
morning, noon, and night.
God looks out to keep me safe,
makes sure that I'm all right.
So I thank you, Lord, and I shout,
    "Praise God."

Let me clap, let me stomp, let me
    spin around now.
I'm safe morning, noon, and night;
God keeps me all right.

God protects me every day,
when I'm far from home.
God is with me even when
I seem all alone.
So I thank you, Lord, and I shout,
    "Praise God."
Let me clap, let me stomp, let me
    spin around now.
Even when I'm far from home,
I am not alone!

Praise God!

## Verse to Say

"With your powerful arm you protect me from every side." *Psalm 139:5, CEV*

## Prayer to pray

Dear God, I know that wherever I am, you will be with me. Amen.

# Our Mighty God

**BIBLE TRUTH**
God is mighty.

**LEARNING FUN**
Initial consonant sound "m"

**SCRIPTURE REFERENCE**
Acts 27, 28

**MEMORY VERSE**
"Who is this King of glory?
The Lord strong and
mighty." *Psalm 24:8, NIV*

Jesus' follower Paul was on a long boat trip. The ship rocked back and forth. Water spilled into the boat. The **m**en were scared.

"God will save us," said Paul. "I believe in a **m**ighty God."

**M**orning came. The ship crashed. Towering waves tossed the **m**en into the sea.

"God will save us," said Paul. "I believe in a **m**ighty God."

The **m**en drifted to an island. The island people served a **m**eal. And Paul reminded the **m**en, "Our **m**ighty God saved us."

**M**onths later, they left the island. The ship sailed **m**any **m**iles. The **m**oment the boat docked, Paul preached, "God cared for us on this long journey. We must tell about our **m**ighty God, and his Son, Jesus."

And that's exactly what Paul did. He welcomed **m**any people into his house. He had traveled **m**any places. Paul gave the same **m**essage everywhere he went. He said, "We have a **m**ighty God. He sent his Son to save us!"

# Activities

Learning to listen for initial consonant sounds, including "m," is only one of many pre-reading skills. Your child has taken many steps toward independent reading as you've worked your way through this book. He has observed that a book is held right-side up, that you read from left to right and front to back. He has watched you look at squiggles on a page that have meaning. Your child has listened to your language patterns and heard the rhythm of your speech. But even more important than the academic skills you have taught by reading this book to your child, you have shared God's story.

## Game to **play**

*Clap every time you hear the "m" sound at the beginning of a word. Encourage your child to do the same.*

Cows moo.
Horses neigh.
Moles tunnel.
Lions roar.
Bats fly.
Monkeys climb.
Crocodiles yawn.
Kittens meow.
Moths flutter.
Owls hoot.
Mice squeak.

## Questions to ask

*Tell your child that Paul told many people about Jesus. But Paul isn't here to do that anymore. Now it is our turn to share the good news that Jesus is our Savior.*

Who was the first person who told you about Jesus?
What is your favorite story about Jesus?
Who can you tell about Jesus?
What are ways people can see that you love Jesus?

## Verse to say

"Who is this King of glory? The Lord strong and mighty." *Psalm 24:8, NIV*

## Prayer to pray

Dear God, you are mighty. I am glad you are my mighty God. You are strong. I am glad you are my strong God. I know you can do anything. Amen.

# Verses to Say

Each "Verse to say" has been selected as an appropriate memory verse for your child—and you! Keep track of the verses your child has memorized in the list below. You may memorize from the Bible versions used in this book, or another version your family prefers.

| | |
|---|---|
| Acts 17:24 | Isaiah 9:6 |
| Nahum 1:7 | Mark 16:15 |
| Psalm 48:1 | Psalm 8:3 |
| 1 Kings 8:20 | Luke 2:40 |
| Proverbs 15:29 | Psalm 136:4 |
| Psalm 46:11 | Psalm 118:7 |
| Job 37:5 | Psalm 119:101 |
| Psalm 125:2 | Matthew 28:19 |
| Psalm 34:15 | Psalm 145:15 |
| 2 Corinthians 9:8 | Romans 13:1 |
| Psalm 37:39 | 1 John 4:16 |
| Judges 5:3 | 1 John 3:18 |
| Jeremiah 29:11 | Psalm 46:10 |
| Psalm 89:8 | Psalm 100:4 |
| Proverbs 3:27 | Psalm 103:3 |
| Psalm 95:2 | Proverbs 8:33 |
| James 1:5 | Daniel 4:37 |
| Proverbs 3:5 | John 13:15 |
| Psalm 68:34 | Mark 15:39 |
| 1 Peter 5:7 | Matthew 28:20 |
| Deuteronomy 7:9 | Acts 1:11 |
| 1 Peter 1:25 | 1 Peter 1:3 |
| Psalm 33:20 | Psalm 40:3 |
| Exodus 20:3 | John 8:47 |
| Jonah 2:2 | Psalm 139:5 |
| John 17:17 | Psalm 24:8 |

## About the author

Dr. Mary Manz Simon earned a doctorate in education from St. Louis University. Named "one of America's top parenting pros" by McCall's magazine, Mary hosts her own syndicated daily radio program, "Front Porch Parenting," which airs on 300 radio stations around the world. Her expertise on better parenting makes her a popular magazine columnist and keynote speaker. Mary, a mother of three, offers "expert advice from a friendly shoulder." Her books have sold more than 1.5 million copies and are available in nine languages.

To find out more, visit her web site at www.marymanzsimon.com

## About the artist

Piers Harper lives in Cumbria, North West England, and holds a degree in Ancient History and Classical Civilization. He has been working as an illustrator for ten years, working in watercolors, inks, and even digital art. Piers has illustrated picture books and educational material covering a wide range of subjects, but his favorite creations are puzzle books which he writes and illustrates.